DANT ZIGK

echt Ste Rathaus

Ko. Artus Hof   H. Spey-   Kon. Ma. Lefimen   H. Roggen haus   S. Barbara Hospital
                 nious haus

BEAUTIFUL
HISTORIC
GDAŃSK

dańsk is only a few years away from celebrating the one thousandth anniversary of its appearance in history. The first record was made in Rome, most probably in 999 by the historian Jan Kanapariusz who, in "The Life of St. Adalbert", wrote for future generations that "in 997 St. Adalbert first came to Gdańsk where he baptised masses of people". As history states, this Prague bishop from the noble stock of Sławnikowce set out from the distant town of Gniezno, his aim was to get to the north-eastern end of Bolesław Chrobry's domain, and to undertake missionary activities among the Prussians. He was accompanied by a team of thirty knights. They did not provide sufficient protection and subsequently he fell under the blows of the Prussians when he found himself in their territory. Soon afterwards he was recognized as a saint and became the patron of Poland, at which time "urbs Gyddanyzc", the city of Gdańsk, appeared in recorded history.

The closer we come to the jubilee the more people will pose questions such as: how was it in the beginning, and how was it later? Our story will not solve everything. Sufficient explanations, including unavoidable hypotheses connected with the past, can be found in excellent historical monographs of Gdańsk; there are also numerous works popularizing the long history of this city, which was full of hardships and dramatic events for many generations. The intention of the authors of this album is to illustrate what the past ten centuries handed down for posterity, as we enter the twenty-first century. Architecture and building will be given voice. These are the places of human activities which not only assist in the organization of life, forming the city world, but also convey information. They reveal the style and standard of home and community life, the improvement of building techniques and the development of the concept of interior design. They express the aesthetic opinions and ambitions of the founders, and very often show their aspiration to amaze neighbours, and newcomers from distant countries. The task of the photographers is to present the attractiveness of Gdańsk buildings, to enable the discovery of their beauty by those who know it well, and to portray the buildings from a different angle or in a slightly different light in order to remind us of the old truth that every city can be rediscovered again and again. The works of the last half-century are also included here since this period makes a very important contribution to the history of Gdańsk.

The concern of the introduction is to support the study with information and commentaries. It will therefore be necessary to refer to the history of the city although it is not the author's intention to summarize it. Only some events and important people, together with their opinions, will be recalled so that the reader may have a wider perspective from which to penetrate the world of historical Gdańsk. The album is addressed to all people who are making their acquaintance with the city on the Motława, to help them open their hearts to this exceptional place.

eople living at the end of the twentieth century are not surprised by the ten years' investment process of constructing towns, and the even shorter period of building several thousand districts they consider normal. They regard, quite rightly, modern building technology together with all its possibilities, and town and country planning, as a means of raising living standards. Gdańsk could not have been founded if there had not been at least two hundred years of development of dispersed settlements in Gdańsk Upland in the 7th and 8th centuries. That much time was necessary for population growth, for the improvement of building and manufacturing techniques, for the gradual movement of settlements towards the bay, and to develop the ability to coexist with the sea. A very important factor, in the microscale, was taking possession of the mouth of the Oder by Mieszko I, and seizing the mouth of the Vistula, on the border with the dominion of the Prussians, by Bolesław Chrobry's army. On the waterlogged areas where the stream of the Motława discharged its water into the Vistula, the

Gdańsk on the Vistula and on the Baltic

The Church of St. Nicholas

mainstay of the Polish country was located in the years 970-990. It was a city with a port, and the seat of the local ruler, separated by an embankment.

Archaeological research discovered the bases of tremendous wooden and earthen embankments together with wharves used by the ruler and the inhabitants of the fishing and craft district. St. Adalbert stayed in this city in 997, and the number of buildings allowed the historian to use the term "urbs" -city. Among numerous objects of those times which are exhibited in the Gdańsk Archaeological Museum there is a big wooden cross, typical of the missionary ceremonies.

At that time there also existed a fortified settlement within the area of today's Long Market (Długi Targ). It also had its own harbour on the site of the crossing of the Motława. This is the place where in the first quarter of the 13th century there appeared settlers from Lübeck, enriching the local Slavonic and Prussian population with the third, German factor.

The local rulers of Gdańsk town were becaming lieutenants of Polish princes and kings, and in the course of time the Gdańsk-Pomeranian prince's dynasty emerged. In 1180 its representative, Sambor I, moved the Cistercian convent to his dominions in Oliva. In 1227 Prince Świętopełk transferred the church of St. Nicholas from the local market to the Dominican Friars' convent in Cracow. This fact created the need for constructing a new parish church (dedicated to St. Catherine). This is the first evidence of the developing urbanization of Gdańsk.

However, it would be a mistake to suppose that those separate settlements were aiming at integration, at the creation of a common urban organism. In the 13th and the beginning of the 14th century, in the area between Ogarna Street and Heweliusza Street, there were at least four such settlements: a craft and merchant settlement in the region of Long Market (Długi Targ) developing in the direction of Holy Ghost Street (Św. Ducha), dominated by Lübeck settlers; a merchant settlement by St.

Nicholas's church; a craft settlement around St. Catherine's church, and the fourth settlement — the prince's town with a borough, surrounded by a common, tall embankment. This was connected by a bridge with the merchant settlement nearby. All the above mentioned abodes were surrounded by waterlogged meadows, swamp or simply lakes and streams. The buildings with almost all wooden-frame constructions filled with clay were undoubtedly scarce. The discoveries made during researches proved that the churches were already built of brick. They were small buildings whose fragments were uncovered in the foundations of later churches. A favourable factor for the development of the city was a trade route from the south towards the shore of the bay at the foot of the Gdańsk Upland (Wysoczyzna Gdańska). It was connected with local roads leading towards the prince's town and the ford across the Motława. The town port was used not only for fishing purposes but also for Baltic trade.

In the 13th century Prince Świętopełk gave urban rights to the inhabitants of the region of St. Catherine's church, and in the years 1257-63 he confirmed rights on the settlement of the Lübeck people by Long Market (Długi Targ). It was an important step towards further development. The elements of municipal government and law were introduced, the rights of the owners of plots of grounds and buildings were legalized. Without doubt the Gdańsk rulers were very much concerned about expanding their domination over the Pomeranian area, which was strengthening its position among the duchies of Poland. The main seat of the duke and his court was still in Gdańsk town, situated in the place which is now surrounded by Grodzka, Rycerska, Na Dylach and Sukiennicza streets, which was visited by St. Adalbert in 997. It is probably the site, where the Romanesque church, whose stone bases were found during archaeological surveys, was constructed.

The Cistercians brought to Oliva by the Gdańsk liege lords in 1180 introduced new, more efficient methods of land cultivation. Damming up the water of the Oliva Stream (Potok Oliwski) they began constructing numerous mills, fulleries and forges. They built their first chapel of timber, but by about 1200 they had already started a brick temple. The northern aisle of the Oliva cathedral, narrow, with richly profiled columns, is a relic of the earliest brick church from the second quarter of the 13th century.

Records of attacks by the Prussians on the Oliva Cistercians, of the burning of their buildings, and beheading monks in the first half of the 13th century explain the defensive character of the Gdańsk settlements. The presence of the Cistercian builders in the 13th century lets us think that the ruler of Gdańsk town was also interested in the introduction of brick. In 1148 there is a record "Castrum Kdanzc in Pomerania" — Gdańsk Castle in Pomerania. And there was much to defend in Gdańsk in the early Middle Ages. During the time of Bolesław Chrobry it was the most important fortress on the north-eastern fringe of this young country. The aim in the times of the district dispersal was to maintain control over the lands close to the Prussian border and to impose domination in Pomerania. The latter was the reason for subordinating the local church organization to the Włocławek bishopric. The Gdańsk forces protected the port ensuring the development of foreign trade, and guarded the mouth of the Vistula whose main stream still flowed this way. Świętopełk, confirmed in 1217 by Leszek Biały (Leszek the White) in Cracow as a lieutenant, in the beginning used the title "By God's Grace the Lord in Gdańsk" and only with time, the title of duke.

When in 1308 Brandenburgian troops invaded Gdańsk Pomerania they were not met with strong resistance and started conquering the town. The highest Pomeranian judge, Bogusza, obtained approval from Władysław Łokietek to call the Teutonic Knights ("King's friends", as they were described in a document of that time) for help. The invaders withdrew, pushed by the monastic forces. The "King's friends" occupied the city and entered the town. During the night of November 13th the Teutonic Knights beheaded the garrison, the Pomeranian Knighthood living in the borough and some of the inhabitants. Hence started the reign of the Teutonic Knights which was to last 145 years. It was important for the further development of Gdańsk that the procedure of law was undertaken in order to regain Gdańsk Pomerania, but it did not bring the expected results; neither did the longlasting war conducted by Władysław Łokietek bring any changes in the arrangement of forces. Eventually Kazimierz the Great (Kazimierz Wielki) acknowledged the situation and in 1343 made peace with the Teutonic Knights.

Only now were stable conditions for the development of Gdańsk set down. In the same year the parish church of St. Mary was erected. The process of bestowing urban rights, based on the Chełm model, was accomplished in 1346, delimiting the Main Town. A network of streets was laid down on the principle of directing main communication routes from land to the port on the east-west axis. They were connected transversely with a net of narrower, auxiliary roads. The curve of Długa Street (Long Street) is undoubtedly the result of subordinating its course to the existing arrangement of houses. There are more concessions of this type to be found in the plan of the Main Town. It is quite natural, taking into consideration that this area had already been inhabited for several centuries. It is worthwhile mentioning that archaeological research on the foundations of the Town Hall proved it was built on the remains of a settlement going back to the 7th — 8th centuries. As early as the 14th century the regulation of the oval form of the Long Market (Długi Targ) was made, giving the shape lasting until today.

The far-sighted imagination of the authors of the foundation act should be appreciated. Demarcating the area of 42 ha of the Main Town gave the possibility of long-term development. A hypothesis might be accepted that already in that time people were aware of the potential possibilities of the sea-port at the mouth of the Vistula.

The Order, having occupied the duke's town in 1308, only after thirty years undertook the bricklaying of the castle. Assuredly, this happened when there had appeared the possibility of making peace with Poland. The Gdańsk Commander was then Winrych von Kniprode, an outstanding personality of the Order, the future Grand

Port on the Motława

Master. A large block of typical, monastic military buildings filled the ground within the Rycerska, Czopowa, Sukiennicza and Grodzka streets of today. Only a fragment of the Swan Tower (Baszta Łabędź), close to the Fish Market (Targ Rybny), and a part of the wall of the castle approaches remained above ground. Building of the Commander's fortification outdistanced the foundation of the Main Town.

In spite of the Main Town which took on a leading role, in 1377 urban rights were given to the craft settlement around St. Catherine's church. It received the name of the Old Town. To the north of it an entirely new Young Town was founded (1380). Soon after 1308 the Slavonic population moved to Osiek. The curve of Osiek Street is regarded as the relic of the border of the oval arrangement of this settlement's building. The other bank of the Motława and Long Gardens (Długie Ogrody) were gradually being populated. Gdańsk settlement agglomerations of the 14th century took up 200 hectares. It was an important undertaking of the Order to change the flow of the Radunia into the channel from Pruszcz, in this way not only providing the city with water but also driving the mill mechanisms.

The construction of the city wall started immediately after the receipt of the foundation document. The wall not only served for defence purposes, but also enabled the control of people's migration thanks to the guards and to closing the gates. The earliest wall was low and from about 1370 was being increased in height, and in the southern and western section it was doubled. A wide moat filled with water constituted additional reinforcement of the defence line from the Upland side. This way, across the bridges over waters, through the stone "neck of transit" between the Prison Tower (Wieżą Więzienną) and the House of Torture (Katownia) led the main entrance to the city, to Długa Street (Long Street). Seven land gates and eight gates on the Motława closed the streets. Over 20 turrets constituted additional reinforcement of the defence. The High, octahedral Jack Tower (Wieża Jacek) dominated the north-west corner, and the Corner Turret (Baszta Narożna) accentuated the link between the southern curtain of the wall and the western.

It is presumed that a complete continuum of the city wall was not constructed from the Motława side. As regards the land gates, there remain only the reconstructed House of Torture (Katownia) and the Prison Tower (Wieża Więzienna). The riverside gates survived in a better state, although there remain only four of the original mediaeval gates: Chlebnicka (the oldest, with the Teutonic coat of arms of the town, 2nd quarter of the 15th century), the Crane (Żuraw) and Mariacka and Straganiarska Streets. Nowadays separated from the water by the wide promenade of the Long Riverside (Długie Pobrzeże), and adapted in the past centuries for residential purposes they lost their defensive character. At first wooden piers for mooring merchant ships were added to them. The Mariacka and Straganiarska Gates were constructed in the last quarter of the 15th century and they are distinguishable because of the decorative appearance of the facades and heraldic compositions. Unquestionably the Crane (Żuraw) closing the Wide Street (Szeroka) is the most important water gate. It was erected in the years 1442-44 on the site of an earlier building, against the protest of the Commander who did not approve of such an enormous project. The Crane became the symbol of Gdańsk and, besides St. Mary's church, the best known brick-built testimony to the history of the town on the Motława. In 1945 it was seriously damaged, even a part of the walls of the turrets (nearly 3 metres thick at ground level) fell down. During reconstruction, the missing fragments were rebuilt, together with the middle, wooden part. It contains the crane machinery.

After the foundation of the town in 1346, brick buildings developed rapidly. Ceramics had been used until then mainly for foundations, cellar walls or the so called fire partitions between buildings, for outer furnace bodies or constructing chimneys. And now, besides the brick defence curb, the construction of the parish church, the

Das recht Stadtsche Rahthaus.

The Main Town Hall

Town Hall and Artus Court (Dwór Artusa) began. It became necessary to organize several dozen brickyards and lime kilns, not forgetting efficient transport.

Simultaneously, piers for mooring ships and work on the water line in the direction of the sea were undertaken. There appeared the necessity of providing materials and labour for the great complex of the castle and its borough. Hundreds of new houses were being erected, and existing buildings were being reconstructed (mainly increased in height). Large cellars, characteristic of Baltic houses, and upper storeys served as stores of goods and materials necessary for the functioning of craft shops. Specialized warehouses and the building of the Granary Island appeared later.

The above mentioned supplies for the Gdańsk Commandery also comprised the maintenance of numerous troops and additional services in the form of various taxes for the needs of the monastic community. Conflicts started to arise out of the worldy discrepancies between the inhabitants and the Order, and of the self-governmental aspirations among the constantly increasing Gdańsk population. The extent of these conflicts increased with the passing of time, and with the improvement of the organizational skills of the craft guilds and townspeople's brotherhoods.

A serious increase in the number of inhabitants during the reigns of the Teutonic Knights resulted to a great extent from favourable conditions of development. They were created by the improved port on the Motława, connected with the Vistula. The floating of agricultural products down the river significantly diminished costs. There remained a vast unbuilt area within the city wall. Intensive settlement of the Żuławy area not only opened a big market for town trade and craft but also constituted a demographic base for the vigorous city. In 1373 Gdańsk held the reunion of the Hanseatic towns and at least from then it was a member of this powerful organization. In proportion to the growing economic potential the representatives of the Gdańsk Council played a more and more important role in the union of the towns supported during Hanseatic assemblies with the votes of delegations from the Prussian Union. The town took advantage of numerous conveniences. Among other things Gdańsk merchants made use of the Hanza's counting houses, scattered all over Europe, which significantly helped commercial contacts and bank operations. Their ships were entitled to discounts in port charges and customs duty. The number of six hundred Gdańsk vessels registered in 1416 proves not only an abrupt change in the economic development of the city's structure, it also gives an idea of the shipowners' profits in the Hanseatic port region.

Besides the works of the defence system there were two very important buildings in each city: a town hall and a parish church. The town hall, as the site of the council's and jury's debates constituted the centre of the commune's government and was also its architectural symbol. It comprised not only the conference rooms of both of the above mentioned bodies but also a treasury with the town's coffers and financial documentation, and a registry, a very important room were the documents of acquired privileges were kept together with the documents of the local government, chronicles, books of the land registry, records of mortgages, judicial documentation etc. Usually the weight and measurement standards were also kept in the Town Hall and there was also a guardroom of the municipal guard in this building.

A new town hall was built in the years 1379-82 on the spot of the previous one,

St. Mary's Church

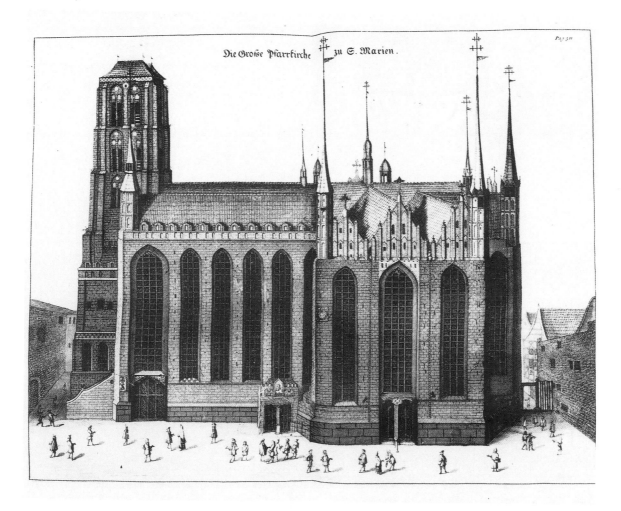

The Interior of Artus Court

where Długa Street (Long Street) changes into Długi Targ (Long Market). It was too modest, did not satisfy the ambitions and future needs, and in addition to that it had no tower because the Gdańsk Commander did not want it to overlook the castle's tower. However, the council ordered the construction of foundations and lower storeys which would stand the weight of a much higher structure. When the Thirteen Years' War ended and Gdańsk liberated itself from the burdensome dependence on the Order, in the second half of the 15th century the tower was not only increased in height by one storey but in 1492 a high tower, with delicate panels, ascended towards the sky. The Town Hall was ornamented from the side of Długi Targ (Long Market) by the decorative wall of an attic enclosed with little towers. One hundred years later the town hall was developed as a whole.

The history of building St. Mary's parish church did not differ much. Laying a corner stone in the year of making peace between the Teutonic Knights and Poland (1343) initiated the building of the high basilica with the tower not much taller than the roof ridge (also in accordance with the Commander's injunction). About thirty years later the church, already finished, seemed inappropriate to the ambitions and material opportunities of the commune, and expressed neither the earnestness of their faith nor the need to impose on other Hanseatic cities. In 1379 a contract with master Ungeradin was signed and there started the erection of transepts and chancel of a hall-like spatial arrangement. Actually it meant building a practically new, much bigger and higher church. When in 1502 the work was finished, a monumental mass with a huge tower dominated the town. It had enough room not only for all the inhabitants of Gdańsk but

The Big Mill

also several thousand newcomers. Yet nearby the parish church of St. John had been functioning for several dozen years. Flooded with light, the surprisingly spacious interior of the church was filled with outstanding pieces of art. The St. Mary's Concathedral Basilica (it was raised to this title in 1986 by a decree of the Congregation of Bishops' Matters) is a significant and convincing example of the historical continuum.

The constant development of the city's economy was accompanied in the 15th century by the growth of the number of inhabitants. The hard-line policy of the Order strongly opposed the clear aspirations for broadening the City Council's rights to self — government. Gdańsk's participation in the anti-Teutonic confederation of Prussia's cities and states, created in 1440, was a logical consequence of this situation. When the Prussian Union's Council decided to take up an armed fight, the Gdańsk delegation met Kazimierz Jagiellończyk for talks. In 1454 an uprising broke out and the Gdańsk Commander gave up the castle to the Council without a fight. The castle was immediately razed to the ground. Several weeks later, on March 6th, the king's Incorporating Act restored Gdańsk to Poland. This union lasted until the second partition of Poland in 1793.

The Thirteen Years' War (1456-64) caused serious casualties and weakened the town's treasury. Kazimierz Jagiellończyk granted special rights to Gdańsk, giving it several privileges. Situated within the borders of the Polish Kingdom, the Gdańsk Council was subordinate only to the monarch. Admittedly the king appointed a

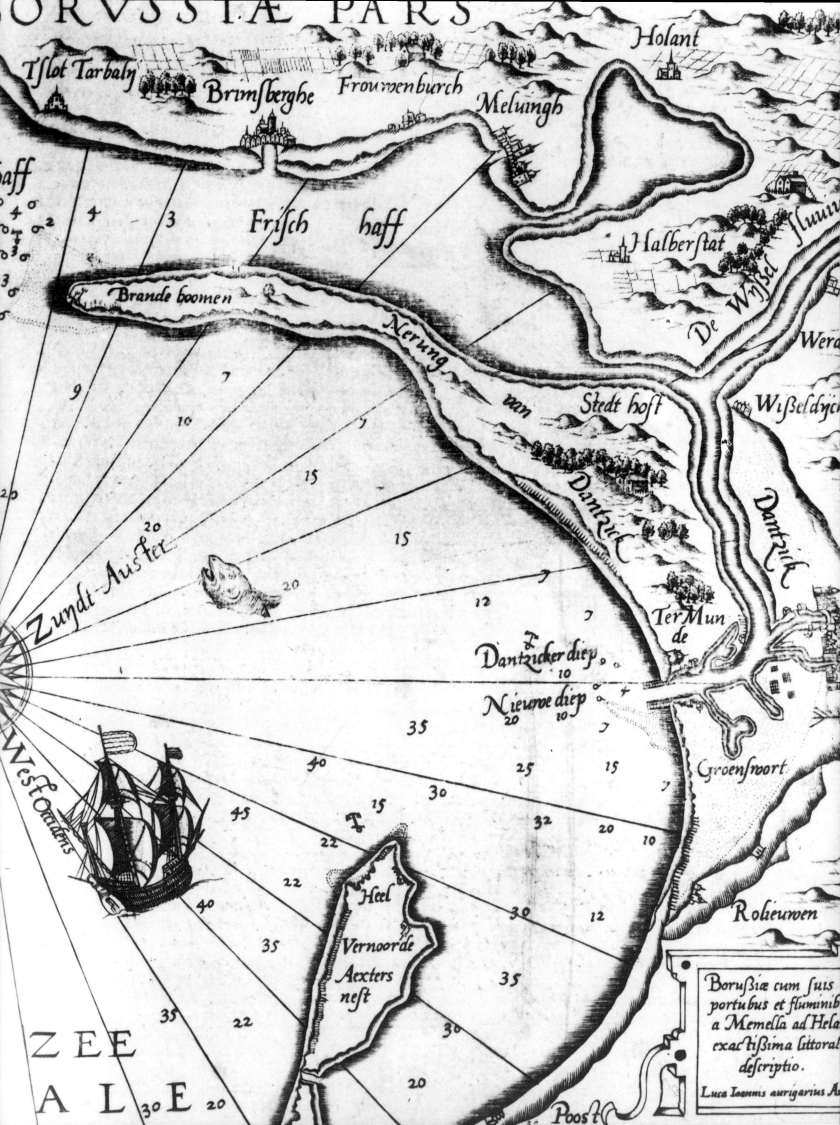

BORVSSIÆ PARS

Tslot Tarbaly Brimsberghe Frouwenburch Meluingh Holant

haff 4 3 Frisch haff

Brande boomen

Nerung

Halberstat

De Wysiel fluui

Wera

Wisseldyck

van Stedt hoft

9 7

10 ,

15

Zundt Auster

20

20

Dantuck

Dantuck

20

15

7

12 7

TerMun de

Dantzicker diep 9 o

10

Nieuwe diep o +

West Occidens

35

20 10 7

40

25 15 7

30

Groensoort

45 T 15

32 20 10

22

22

Heel

30 12

Vernoorde Aexters nest

Roſieuwen

35

40

35 22

ZEE 30 20

ALE

20

Poost

Boruſſiæ cum suis
portubus et fluminib
a Memella ad Hela
exactiſſima littoral
deſcriptio.

Luca Ioannis aurigarius A

representative, but the tenure lasted only one year and the candidates came from Gdańsk, chosen usually from councillors or mayors. The council acquired the right to impose its own taxes, legal regulations in the city, and, what is most important, Gdańsk gained de facto a monopoly on Polish sea trade. All operations were allowed only through the brokerage of Gdańsk merchants. When in the 16th century the European demand for agricultural products increased dramatically and the rich Republic developed the sea trade, Gdańsk profited from every grain of Polish cereal and every piece of Flemish cloth.

Having once acquired its position, Gdańsk was strengthening it continuously, acquiring new privileges. Linked directly with the Crown, it received acknowledgement of privileges from every king to follow. It was also very often in conflict, sometimes bloody, with the Crown. There were various reasons, but the most crucial was the defence of the form of government. Tumults connected with the Reformation, which came here early because in 1518, domestic fights by the mob and political factions against the Council had already brought about interventions of the royal committees, very often drastic in character. Gdańsk inhabitants dared to plunder and burn the Cistercian house in Oliva, together with the church, and to behead people fighting in the name of the king, or to wheel out their cannons and repel efficiently the siege in 1577. There is no room here to discuss all the examples of conflicts. It has to be loyally admitted, however, that Gdańsk councillors and mayors acted with deliberation and patience even in the most difficult and dramatic situations. During sometimes lengthy negotiations they could calmly remove all the obstacles hindering them on their way to regain the position of the town in the Republic. It is justified to suppose that the substantial financial reserves of the Gdańsk Council helped the rapprochement of the two sides.

There are many facts indicating that this situation was not dictated only by the existing state of affairs and did not result from a temporary predominance of the Polish option in the Council. One of the most spectacular predicaments was to be solved during the two dynastic wars between Poland and Sweden. In both cases (1626 and 1655) the Gdańsk Council did not enter into talks with the invader, in order to keep the neutrality desired by the Swedes. The gates were closed, the artillery was wheeled out on the

Panorama of Gdańsk ab. 1680

The Court of St. George's Brotherhood

embankments and the suburban lowlands were flooded to make the approach difficult. But it did not come to battle, even when the foreign army was conquering Warsaw and taking Cracow. In the winter of 1733/34, when the Polish king Stanisław Leszczyński was sheltered in Gdańsk, escaping from a stronger candidate for the throne, the city survived six months of hard siege. After the king's escape to France it had to make contributions to the vanquishers. This position taken up by Gdańsk resulted from the pragmatic approach to the political reality. The Royal Town's Council defended the reasons of the State, being aware of its decision. The future of this city, hopes for its development or at least maintaining its present position, were all based exclusively on the maintenance of its close and very privileged union with the Republic.

It should be pointed out that at the close of the 15th century Gdańsk already comprised an area much larger than the city agglomeration with the adjacent terrains. The area subordinated to the Council included a part of the Hel peninsula, significant tracts of Żuławy and Mierzeja Wiślana (the Vistula Sand-Bar), and a part of Wyżyna Gdańska (Gdańsk Upland), which all together made an area of 640 square kilometres. As a rightful, although often troublesome, member of the Prussian Council, Gdańsk constituted a part of Royal Prussia and had the right to take part in royal elections. In 1492 a municipal delegation took part in the election for the first time, supporting the candidate of the Prussian states, Jan Olbracht, and in 1506 it voted for Zygmunt I. Participation in this important judiciary act meant not only the performing of duties assigned as a privilege or the fulfilment of the patricians' ambitions. It was also an excellent opportunity to open up personal contacts with the leading personages of the Kingdom, to develop closer relationships, to gain support for various matters and initiatives. This was also the way towards nobility, and high political and church ranks.

he beginning of the 16th century was evidently a period of economic stabilization for Gdańsk. It was supported by the increase of mercantile contacts with Lithuanian-Russian markets facilitated by the Jagiellonian policy. There ended a big building cycle connected with the late medieval initiatives. The town looked beautified with St. Mary's church, the Town Hall, Artus Court, the exclusive Court of St. George's Brotherhood. The modernization of the brick defence system was complete.

Presumably the town was all built up within the city wall. However, the houses of the skeleton construction filled with clay were still in the majority. Only better off patrician families could afford brick facades for their houses and all-brick houses were very rare. A block of buildings belonging to St. Mary's parish was an exception, and the part-stone facade of the house on 15 Chlebnicka Street was absolutely unique. Already in 1455 it was forbidden by municipal law to cover the roofs of houses and annexes with straw or reeds, and another regulation stated that not only male inhabitants but also women and nuns were obliged to put out fires. More and more Gdańsk inhabitants, having been taught in good parish and municipal schools, left for university studies. The time of the Reformation and social revolution was coming, and this is how the Golden Age of Gdańsk was to begin.

The above mentioned journeys to the universities concerned of course young people from the wealthiest families. The Ferbers, settled here for more than a century, belonged to the richest in Gdańsk. In 1463, son Eberhard, one of ten children, was born to Mayor John Ferber. Having finished the best parish school at St. Mary's church, he was polishing his manners at the court of Mecklemburg. He took part in knightly tournaments, and then, as a member of the retinue of Pomeranian Duke Bogusław X, he went on a pilgrimage to Christ's Grave in Jerusalem where he was knighted by the Duke. On arrival in his hometown he took up a very lucrative post

Houses on Długa Street (Long Street)

as an administrator of the Puck district pledged to the city by the Crown. Several years later he administered the whole of Gdańsk Żuławy. He became Mayor in 1510, and was appointed burgrave in 1512 by Zygmunt I. He accompanied the king to the kings' reunions in Preshburg (Bratislava) and Vienna in 1515. For his merits he received for life four villages in Żuławy which had been held on lease until then, and the Tczew district. It is probably to him that we owe the Renaissance portal of 1517 made in Wawel's workshop of Italian sculptors; presently the portal may be admired in the hallway of the Old Town's Town Hall. Debarred from posts of authority during the social riots in 1520, he was again, for the tenth time, appointed to the post of burgrave five years later. Having experienced satisfaction over the town society he withdrew to his Tczew district.

K onstantin, one of ten sons of Eberhardt, as a mayor became a burgrave for the first time in 1557. He was a representative of a modern generation of patricians. Running a big commercial enterprise he used his capital buying or renting landed properties. He settled the Dutch on his lands, modernized the economy and erected industrial plants. He was a banker of Zygmunt August and Zygmunt III Waza. He astonished and teased his contemporaries not only because he wore a heavy gold chain all the time, but also because he used to go about his hometown in a cart drawn by six horses. Having reached in 1557 the highest post in the city he decided to take his old family house on 28 Długa Street to pieces and build a modern palace-like seat, which was actually finished in 1560. It was the first modern house in town, quite different from the others existing until then. An unknown builder erected a classical Renaissance facade, almost completely covered with stone. Delicate pilasters show three axes, and profiled cornices frame richly-sculpted friezes, dividing the facades into storeys which become smaller and smaller towards the top. There are six heads of ancient heroes

A Chamber in the Main Town Hall

A Hall in the Lions' Castle

leaning out of the friezes, and the upper frieze, the attic, includes the coats of arms: of the Republic (placed by mistake on the side during the reconstruction), of Royal Prussia, and of Gdańsk. It is a unique example of a family house facade with a kind of heraldic composition found only on municipal buildings. The whole is surmounted by sculptures of men in ancient garments, standing on the axis of the pilasters. For the first time in a Gdańsk house, rectangular windows were introduced, which reduce the surface of the wall. We do not have descriptions of an old representative hallway which became the prototype for the next to be built. None of the later historical houses, even though often bigger or more magnificent or richer in ornaments, could equal the artistic standing and elegance of the Ferberian ambition.

I do not mention ambition accidentally. It had been expressed in Gdańsk for a long time in numerous artistic foundations. In the first quarter of the century, at the beginning of the Reformation, there appeared in St. Mary's church outstanding Flemish altars from Antwerp and Mechelen. Master Michael was brought from Augsburg to make the main altar. In the road arch of the temple Master Paul placed an excellent Passion of enormous dimensions. Just when the emotions of the first years of the Reformation weakened, the masterpieces of painting, sculpture and wood-carving, founded by competing brotherhoods of the town, decorated the walls of Artus Court. There came the time of architecture and building in the 16th century. This was now the area to express individual and common ambitions. A significant number of the patrician families did not have to be engaged in trade by then. They became financiers, the owners of vast landed properties.

The building of Ferber's Renaissance house on Długa Street (Long Street) became a challenge for other patrician families. Undoubtedly it was the time when the

The Green Gate

Konerts, the owners of the industrial plants on the Potok Oliwski (Oliva Stream), the founders of the outstanding pieces of fine arts, built their seat on Długa Street (Long Street). A dozen or so competing family houses appeared in the Old Town. They prove that the controversy over the primacy between two artistic orientations, Italian Renaissance and Netherlandic mannerism was finally settled by the artists brought to Gdańsk by the Council. Thus the Mayors and councillors played a decisive role in artistic matters. There are numerous examples proving this state of affairs.

In 1565 Hans Kramer, a builder belonging to the court of the Saxonic elect in Dresden, known also because of his works in Wittenberg and Freiberg, accepted the post of municipal builder. In 1586 two equally distinquished Flemish artists from Mechelen settled in Gdańsk: the architect Anton van Obberghen, famous for the development of the king's fortress and a castle in Kronborg on the Sund, which he built for King Frederick II, was given the post of municipal builder, and Wilhelm van den Blocke, an outstanding sculptor, known through his works for the duke's court in Królewiec and for the royal family of Batory. He also kept to the forms of northern art. The choice of artists brought by distinguished patrons confirms the opinion about the great ambitions and artistic sensibilities of the Gdańsk councillors.

Kramer immortalized his name in the years 1565-70, building the tallest house in town at that time, English House on 16 Chlebnicka Street, and the Lion's Castle on 35 Długa Street (Long Street). He also conducted the building of the royal palace, because this was the appropriation of Zielona Brama (The Green Gate), finished in 1568, closing Długi Targ (Long Market) from the side of The Motława. As an engineer also specializing in designing defence buildings, he began serious defensive earthworks on the western curtain of the town and in the Wisłoujście (Vistula Mouth) fortress. The forms of his works oscillated between the traditional Saxonic models and manneristic decoration, represented by the stonework elements to be found in Zielona Brama (The Green Gate) and its tops. The novelty of the bricks of small dimensions used in the building made an impression on Gdańsk inhabitants. They were called Dutch because they were imported from Amsterdam. Yet it was not a symptom of the Council's prodigality. The majority of the ships from The Netherlands came to Gdańsk without cargo, in order to buy goods — mainly cereal or other agricultural products. The holds were ballasted with the bricks which undoubtedly made the freight cheaper.

Van den Blocke ornamented the main entrance to Gdańsk, Brama Wyżynna (the Upland Gate), with a stone slab facing patterned after one of the Antwerpian municipal gates. Today its neighbours are a neo-Renaissance bank building and a modern glazed pavilion. Having lost its original surrounding, the building stopped being an important element of the western panorama of the city. Originally the defensive earth embankment reached this gate, not exceeding the height of its frieze and a big bridge, which was partly a draw-bridge, enabled movement over a wide moat filled with water. The eagle of the Republic, over the middle arcade of the gate, has a coat of arms of Ciołek on his breast. This is a gem of the last Polish king, Stanisław August Poniatowski. Other excellent works of master Willem, stone epitaphs of Mayor Johannes Brandes and his wife, and of the juror Edward Blemke still decorate St. Mary's church.

The most outstanding modern works were erected in Gdańsk by Anton van Obberghen who came here from Denmark, having finished his king's commission in Kronborg. The Old Town Hall (1586-95) is a gem of Flemish architecture. It is a

The Upland Gate, The Prison Tower

The Old Town Hall

two-storey brick building with two roofs. The corner pinnacles with pointed cupolas not only accentuate the corners but also relieve the monotony of the upper part of the building surmounted by a cupola of carefully determined proportions. Stone window framings, decoratively worked out surfaces of the portal's ashlars and a niche on both its sides, complete the whole. Similarly Wielka Zbrojownia (Great Armoury, 1602-1605) registered van Obberghen for good in the history of the town's art. It is a leading object, quoted in the history of European architecture. The facade, put together with two turrets accentuates and closes the perspective of Piwna Street (Beer Street). Two storeys of big windows were to guarantee day light to the long halls inside. On the lower storey cannons, cannon balls and other heavy war equipment were kept. On the upper floor (accessible by the stairways of both turrets), lighter arms were stored. An attic in the form of decorative gables constituted the third storey. The attic was to cover the roofs. In 1945 Zbrojownia (The Armoury) was burnt-out — the outer walls were the only remnants. After the rebuilding it was appropriated for the seat of the University of Fine Arts. In this way the dreams of the 19th century Gdańsk artists came true: artistic youth received a university in accordance with the needs of the city and the whole region, famous also in the neighbouring Baltic countries. From the side of Targ Węglowy (Coal Market) the Armoury is surrounded by modern buildings — the Wybrzeże (the Seaside) Theatre to the left, with a glazed facade reflecting rich stone decorations of Obberghen's work, and an administrative-didactic building of the University of Fine Arts to the right. There are also two other works of van Obberghen to be seen from Zbrojownia (the Armoury) on Targ Węglowy (Coal Market): Katownia (The House of Torture) whose Gothic mass was modernized by him, and the roof of the Prison Tower, surmounted by a decorative cupola (its reconstruction was finished in 1992).

The Great Armory

The raising of the modern fortifications of the town started from the western side with the building of the brick Brama Wyżynna (The Upland Gate) in the green grass-covered curtain of the embankments. It was soon decided to surround Gdańsk with an enormous stone-and-earth curb of bastions with deep moats filled with water. This big defensive programme ensured the absolute safety of the town - no part of the system was captured, even during sieges of many months. The project was designed by the outstanding Dutch specialist Cornelius van den Bosch who also personally conducted the realization of his plan. The works lasted from 1619 to 1636. In that time the Motława was channelled in a new riverbed, ultimately separating Wyspa Spichrzów (Granary Island). Already then it was completely built up with granaries. It constituted a separate, strictly guarded region inaccessible after dusk. From the 16th century stores of goods and warehouses were being located on the island. Hence the upper storeys of Gdańsk buildings comprised spare bedrooms, living rooms and rooms appropriated for collections of books and art. There appeared annexes in the unbuilt-up plots behind the front doors. The population within the modern fortifications of Gdańsk of the 17th century amounted to about 70 thousand, and the suburban building developed more and more. It was not only a place for those who did not get the municipal right to settle within the embankments. There were more and more patrician families who built their suburban seats in Długie Ogrody (Long Gardens), Wrzeszcz, Oliva or even in Sopot or in Żuławy.

The works of architecture which were to bring fame to their founders were still being built. The Council commissioned the dismantling of the medieval Brama Długouliczna (The Long Street Gate) adjoining Dwór Bractwa Św. Jerzego (the Court of St. George's Brotherhood). Abraham van den Blocke, a sculptor, and Willem's son

The Golden Gate

designed and, together with municipal builder Jerzy Strakowski, erected Brama Złota (The Golden Gate, 1612-1614) on this spot. He combined two opposing artistic orientations in one building: classical character shows itself in the monumental columns accentuating two identical elevations, whereas the stone slab facing is decorated with the motifes of Flemish provenance. Italian and Dutch elements of this orginal work are complementary to one another. The sign on the eastern elevation says, "Small countries grow through harmony, big countries fall through disharmony", and the sign to the side of Wieża Więzienna (The Prison Tower) goes, "May those fare well who love you, may peace prevail within your walls and happiness in your palaces". These words directed to the contemporary and future generations have not yet become out-of-date.

At the same time Złota Kamienica (The Golden House) of Johannes Speimann was built on Długi Targ (Long Market). It was designed in 1609 by Abraham van den Blocke, and Hans Voigt from Rostock finished all sculpture works in 1618, abundantly gilding nearly all reliefs. The pilaster division of the facade comes from the tradition of the Italian Renaissance but the way they are decorated points to a northern source. Multifigural scenes of friezes present important historical events, and they are supplemented by the busts of outstanding personages. In order to avoid mistakes they are all provided with captions — there is Themistocles, Brutus, but also Kazimierz Jagiellończyk. There is a bust of the ruling king Zygmunt III Waza who, at the very same time as Speimann was finishing work on the facade of his house, appointed him, Mayor of Gdańsk, to the post of burgrave enriching his career with greatest splendour. In order not to go into the small details of the achievements of this distinguished inhabitant of Gdańsk, I will add only that in the years 1589-92 he went to Genoa during the dramatic calamity of hunger in the vanguard of the Gdańsk fleet of 25 ships filled with cereal. In token of gratitude the Pope raised him to the rank of nobility of the "Golden Knight". He became councillor in 1603.

Speimann's superexlibris showing him in a suit of armour comes from 1605. He was a respected humanist and an objets d' art collector. He founded a monument in St. Mary's church for his Gdańsk parents-in-law of the Bahrs of Rawicz coat of arms. The monument was the work of Abraham van den Blocke. This big stone monument modelled after tombstones of the families of north European dukes seemed so extravagant to the church council that they refused their consent to its building. The Town Council ended the debate coming out with a verdict according to the burgrave's wishes and the monument has been standing in the northern arm of the transept since 1620, rising high above the heads of the believers the fully plastic figures of the married couple. He stored his equestrian statue in Wielka Zbrojownia (Great Armoury). It was in his residence that Zygmunt III Waza was received in 1623: "they were bathing, dancing, and enjoying themselves until night …" Dying in 1625, Johannes Speimann bequeathed in his will a scholarship for foreign studies to a young man on condition that after his return to Gdańsk the man would become a custodian of the family collection. The collection was to be open to the public once a month free of charge. It is possible to mention many such outstanding, ambitious men of intellect, inhabitants of Gdańsk of that time. His close friend Bartholomeus Schackmann was a co-burgrave and the initiator of the building of Wielka Zbrojownia (Great Armoury), also participating in the erection of Brama Złota (The Golden Gate).

Splendid works of art were left not only by fortune-owners. Scientists, educators, and editors are also recorded for good in the history of Gdańsk. Konrad Baumgard founded a printing house in 1498, while intense activity at Rhode's printing house started in 1538. It is the date of Rhode's edition of two Polish issues: "Abecadło polskie" ("Polish Alphabet") and

The Philosopher Bartholomeus Keckermann

The Historian Reinhold Curicke

25

In the Library of the Academic College

"Ewangelie i Epistoły" ("Gospels and Epistles"). From 1473 two moulding plants started operating. In 1558 Johann Hoppe became the first rector of Gdańsk college. The development of humanities in the Academic College brought about the creation of the Polish language course in 1589, and in 1594 Nicolaus Volckmar edited "Compendium linguae polonicae". He was also an author of the German-Polish conversation manual entitled "Viertzig Dialogi". The Gdańsk inhabitant Bartholomeus Keckermann, a philosopher and historian, created a law and history department at the College. He was one of the first in the world to propose including the history of science, culture and art into the studies. In the 17th century the Academic College enjoyed so high a reputation that its graduates were admitted to the junior year of European universities. Its famous collection of books is kept by the Gdańsk Library of the Polish Academy of Science. Reinhold Curicke, the secretary of the Gdańsk Council belonged to the distinguished graduates of the Gdańsk Atheneum. He is the author of the monograph of Gdańsk of the 17th century "Beschreibung der Stadt Danzig ..." written in 1645. Besides the history of the city based on records, he inserted excellent illustrations and descriptions of the most interesting Gdańsk buildings.

The two Swedish wars of the 17th century resulted in commercial problems but they did not retard the development of architecture, culture or art. Many buildings were ornamented with new facades, stone Baroque decoration and new colouring appeared. The antethresholds started to be more intensively developed and decorated with sculpted stone panels. Outstanding Gdańsk sculptor Andreas Schlüter Junior started his artistic career here before he made himself famous with excellent works in the Berlin armoury. The Royal Chapel (1678-81) was founded by primate Andrew Olszowski and John III Sobieski. It is the only Baroque church in the Main Town, completely influenced by the reformed faith. Aiming at the maintenance of building scale on Św. Ducha Street (Holy Ghost Street) the royal architect Tylman from Gameren designed a quiet, distinctive, pilaster facade with the protuberant cornice covered with a big coat of arms of the Crown, surmounted by a dome on an octagonal tambour. The builder Bartel Ranisch commissioned young Schlütes to make decorative sculptures of the elevation. The interior of the chapel on the second storey also occupies two apartment buildings flanked by the chapel, constituting one original composition.

The links of Jan III Sobieski with Gdańsk were not only official in character. He respected one of the Gdańsk inhabitants particularly. This was the famous astronomer, Jan Heweliusz. A son of the brewer Hewelke, following the contemporary fashion he used his name in Latin transcription, Johannes Hevelius, hence Polonized Heweliusz. He built an astronomic observatory on three roofs of buildings on Korzenna Street (shown in Curicke's work). He himself constructed a big (for that time) telescope, 150 feet long and ground its lenses himself. He printed the results of his observations in the best printing houses of Gdańsk. In 1644, he was the first Gdańsk scientist to become a member of the Royal Society in London. His achievements were appreciated by Louis XIV and Jan III Sobieski, who gave permanent salaries to the astronomer. However, he dedicated the discovered constellation only to his king naming it "Scutum Sobiescianum" (Sobieski's Shield). A popular portrait of Heveliusz, painted by Daniel Schultz, known also from graphic replicas, presents the scientist against the background of the library. One hand is resting on the manuscript, the other touches a globe of constellations. It is a moment of the astronomer's contemplation although he is looking carefully at the viewer. It is first of all a portrait of an explorer of the heavenly bodies, but his clever look remaining in contact with the viewer shows his connection with earthly life. And this is true about Jan Heweliusz who devoted most of his life to the work

The Astronomer Jan Hewelius

A Title Page of Curicke's Chronicle

of the jury and then the council of the Old Town. It is not by chance that such a grand-scale scientist was deeply involved in the social life and matters of his commune. It seems to me that the sensitivity to these problems is an evident feature of the character of the Gdańsk inhabitants, not only of past generations. Heweliusz dedicated to his city one of the fundamental works of his life: "Selenographia", the description of his observation of the Moon (1647). A year before his death, in a modest house in Ogarna Street another Gdańsk inhabitant was born, who was also to contribute significantly to world science: Gabriel Fahrenheit, creator of the thermometric scale.

The 18th century did not bring important changes in the building of this town surrounded by its line of defensive bastions. These bastions also limited development possibilities. The facades of many houses were modernized, new facades being built sporadically. Nevertheless the main works left over from previous centuries were carefully renovated enjoying the memory and imagination of the contemporary inhabitants. They also kept up the local patriotism with the recollection of the power and glory of Gdańsk, which seemed to have faded. Still, the scientific and intellectual life developed intensively. The first of the scientific associations of Gdańsk, "Library Association" was founded in 1720. The Natural Science Association, created in 1743 by Daniel Gralath was of fundamental importance. It conducted scientific research and published its results. It was from its membership that the creation of the Polish Royal Scientific Association came. And although this idea did not receive the approval of the reigning August II Sas, his successor Stanisław August Poniatowski was a member of the Gdańsk association. The king's interest in science and art is widely known but the understanding of Gdańsk researches and initiatives is not by chance. Indeed, young Poniatowski once had as his tutor Gotfryd Lengnich, a well-known historian and professor at

Port on the Motława

Gdańsk Academic College. Among his various dissertations the volume "History of Royal Prussia" should be mentioned together with "Historia Polona a Lecho" ("The History of Poland from Lech"). Along with the weakening of the Polish country Gdańsk inhabitants felt increasing uneasiness. The text of a prayer written in 1772 is good proof of this situation. It was edited by Johannes Scheibler and it was obligatory to read it from the pulpits. "Lord, spread the light of Your visage over the Majesty of the Polish Republic, over our most gracious King and Lord, give him, Oh Lord, Your omnipotent protection and constant care. Give him wisdom, strength, power, health and all that is most favourable. Make him shine in the world out of the darkness and bestow peace and quietude on the Polish Kingdom and the lands connected with it. Stop Your disgrace and comfort us again with Your help".

The beginning of the 19th century brought in 1813 a twelve month siege of the town by the Prussian and Russian armies. Over 1100 houses were seriously damaged or simply destroyed. From then on, independently of the on-going restoration of damage, of municipal regulation activities and modernization, the wisest inhabitants of Gdańsk did their best to protect those elements of the brick history of Gdańsk which still remained untouched. A particular role was played by Johann Carl Schultz, an outstanding engraver, painter and professor at Gdańsk University of Fine Arts. He issued three volumes of copperplates depicting the most important monuments of Gdańsk architecture (1842-67). He founded The Association for the Protection of Buildings and Artistic Monuments, and together with a group of its active members he managed to protect many historical buildings and ante-thresholds (which were then still abundant on the main historical routes) from being taken to pieces. He did not succeed, however, in saving one of the most important towers of the southern part of the fortification, close to the Baszta Narożna (The Corner Tower). No wonder then that during the reconstruction of Gdańsk after 1945, it was rebulit on the same spot according to the drawings of J.C. Schultz and named after him.

der Stadthoff.

The Corner Turret and J.C. Schultz's Turret

esides the questions concerning the past, which I posed at the beginning, it is necessary to formulate other, equally valid questions. To what extent is Gdańsk the continuation of a one thousand years old tradition? This question has already been asked many times although the time and circumstances were not always favourable enough to answer it in a satisfactory way. Teresa Grzybkowska, the author of an inventive book "Golden Age of Gdańsk Painting Against the Background of the Artistic Culture of the City 1520-1620" (1990), aptly formulated the following opinion in the introduction: "Contemporary Gdańsk becomes incomprehensible without the explanatory light of history,which is nothing else but an incessant questioning of the past times in the name of the problems, concerns and misgivings of today". The question about the nature of contemporary continuation in fact concerns modern times. Only while explaining this is it possible to go back. I propose therefore to answer the question about the truth of today, and then about the past.

Undoubtedly Gdańsk continues the achievements of past generations. It is not only because Gdańsk inhabitants live in the same place where 10 centuries ago the generations took pains to create Gyddanyzc. It is not the most important in what period of time and in what transcription the name of the city was used by the majority of inhabitants. It is important however, that the German transcription "Danzig" does not evoke, or should not now evoke, the associations which were for a long time being incited and fixed in our memory.

The past of the city, recorded in documents and preserved in the old material works, constitutes only a part of the modern whole, supplemented by its contemporary population. It should be openly admitted that the latter factor decides everything. Ancient Mycenae is an example of a broken historical continuation.

The name which every enlightened European associates with great memorable events. Countless crowds of tourists coming there find only valuable ruins, beautiful Greek landscape and... their own historical associations which made them come to this place.

Contemporary Gdańsk constitutes a new quality. Nothing reminds us of the smouldering ruins of March 30th, 1945. There are nearly no living eye-witnesses of this date. There does not even exist a reasonable number of descendants of Gdańsk Poles, the lack of whom we feel so dramatically. Instead there are newcomers, the majority of whom assuredly could not even imagine living so far from the family landscapes, graves and history. They were helped here by neighbours from the Kashubian region, from the whole of Pomerania and other areas of present-day Poland. Together they made an effort of settling in the place called Gdańsk. They put down the roots of their hopes and started to rebuild the city.

Before that they took out two million cubic metres of debris from the terrain of the Main Town, which is comparable with the volume of the Great Pyramid in Gizeh. They believed that it was possible to start living here anew. Moreover, they engaged themselves in a whole-hearted effort to save the relics of the past which, in these pioneer times, were waiting for salvation. Many of them learned only here what Gdańsk was. It was not learning from books and stories. They were gripped by the eagles of the Republic, preserved here in abundance. The archaeologist had also much to tell, having dug deep into the slimy ground, efficiently looking for the roots of urbs Gyddanyzc.

This great demographic experiment of creating a new municipal society in the place which was nearly a desert could turn out to be a failure, the more so as it had not been planned but was a side effect of great historical processes. It was, however, a success and there is no doubt about it, because the third generation of Gdańsk inhabitants, no longer newcomers, is coming to life. Their grandfathers and fathers managed to protect from irretrievable loss a large part of the material heritage of their predecessors. Where this was impossible they re-created the buildings on a previously unknown scale, on an area of 42 hectares. And suddenly it appeared that the town erected by them, to a large extent contemporary, became a link with the past — they felt proper successors of the old inhabitants of Gdańsk.

It is enough to look at the trees and bushes planted by the inhabitants of Mariacka Street on their own initiative, in order to live better on their street. But it is necessary to find out how many old works of art belonging to St. Mary's Cathedral Basilica were preserved by the funds of the parishioners to be sure that they consciously continue the Gdańsk tradition. St. Mary's parish priest convinces people of this truth, informing us that he is the sixtieth priest in this place after Conrad who started the work in 1334. It is worthwhile knowing the understanding with which the initiatives of Gdańsk inhabitants living abroad were accepted in preservation works in Gdańsk. I do not know how many sincere friends Günter Grass, born in Wrzeszcz, has outside Gdańsk, but I know that here he has many.

Do the inhabitants of Gdańsk differ much from their predecessors ? Is there anything that may be called the Gdańsk character ? Probably yes. Although far fewer inhabitants are connected with work on the sea today, a similar situation is in Lübeck, Stockholm or Tallin. They certainly can, as their predecessors could, work hard and efficiently, and also, like those people, they are aware of how much reaches their pocket.

There probably exists a Gdańsk genius loci because, like those from previous ages, they possess an inborn sense of dignity, justice, and they are not humble. And in dealing with an important matter they can be stubborn and uncompromising.

Gdańsk history shows that the process of the continuation of the forefathers' achievements has been kept up here for over one thousand years. This process has been broken several times but there were always persistent people there who belonged to the good tradition of Gdańsk. Therefore, when the reader contemplates this dilemma I insist on trying to solve it in accordance with their own knowledge and point of view because Gdańsk deserves it.

17th Century Gdańsk Coat of Arms

Fot.
2

Fot.
8

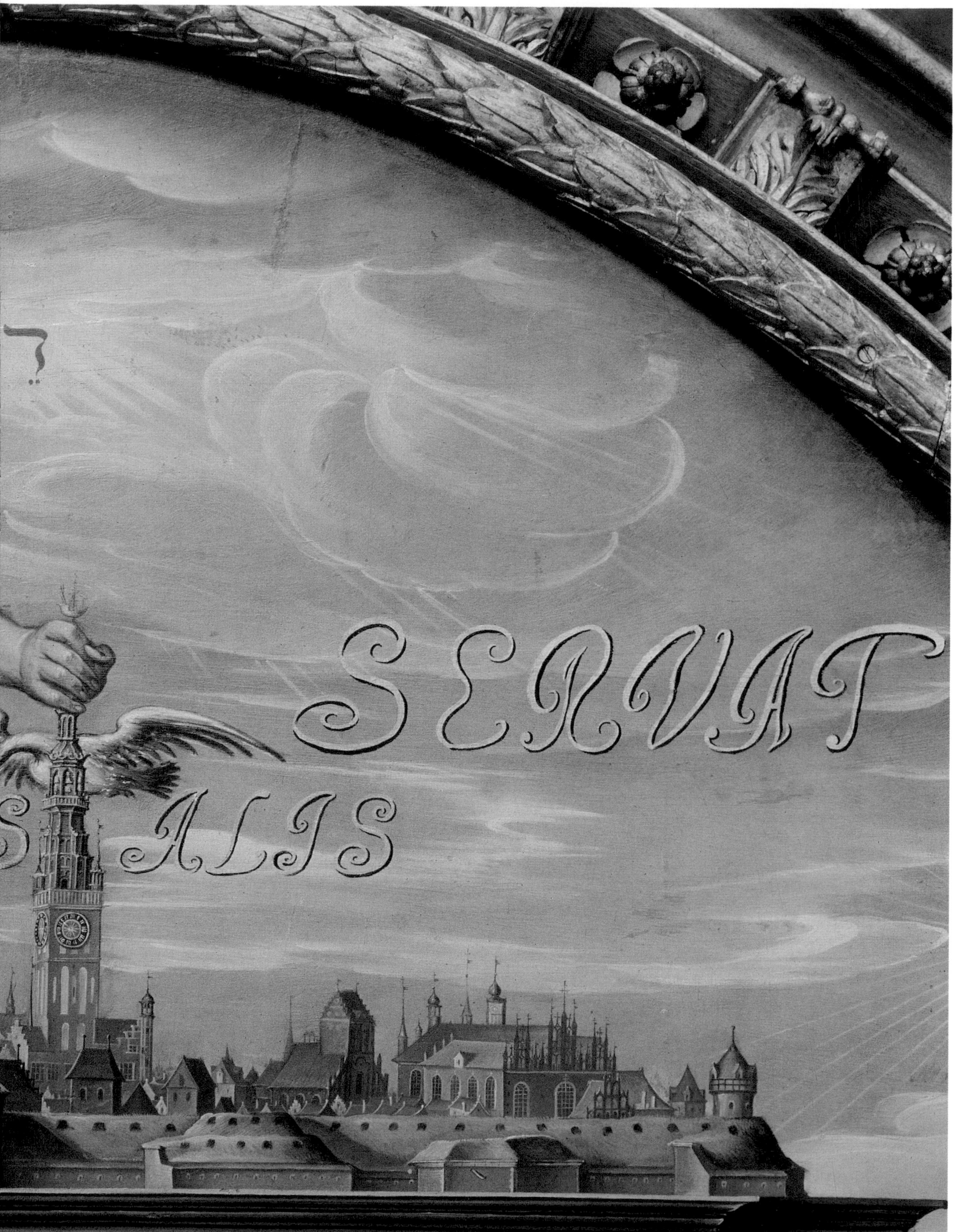
SERVAT
ALIS

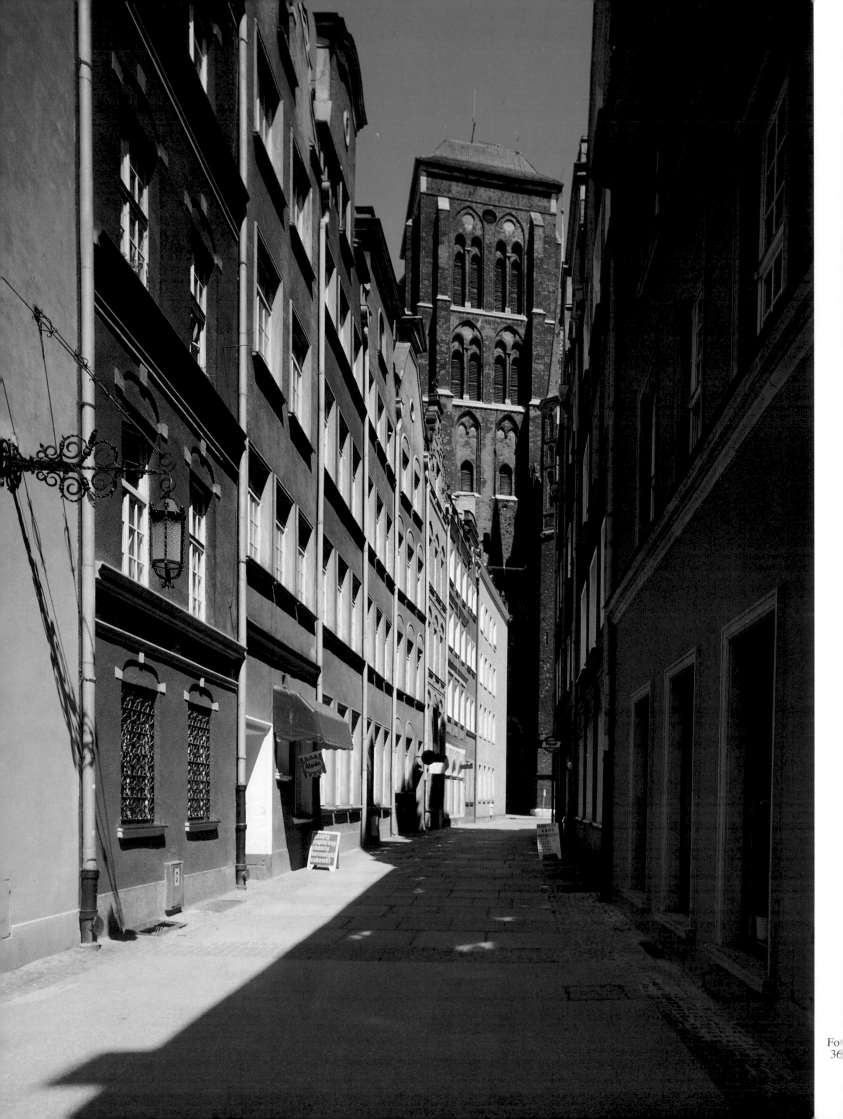

Fot.
38

Fot.
66

Fot.
67

Fot.
88

JAN III SOBIESKI

1629 ✦ 1696

Fot.
94

ABOUT THE ILLUSTRATIONS

1

From the dawn of its history Gdańsk has been a port. The main artery, where the life of the inhabitants, people poised between the land and sea, pulsed and blazed in all its resourcefulness, lay along the banks of the Motława where it flowed into the Vistula just before the waters of both rivers reach the Baltic Sea. The last meanderings of both rivers shield the port from storms and ·make the haven a calm one (c.f. illustration 84 and the maps reproduced in this album). As we look up the Motława river, we can see on the left the partially reconstructed row of granaries on Granary Island and on the right, dominating the landing-stage known as the Long Riverside, the Crane, a massive building now joined to the Bridge Gate (c.f. illustration 9 and Aegidius Dickman's engraving from his "Praecipuorum locorum et aedificiorum quae in urbe Dantiscana visuntur adumbratio", an album of views of Gdańsk published in 1617, which can be seen on p. 8). Nowadays cargo ships do not call here - the docks and the landing-stages now occupy the banks of the Vistula at its mouth, and even the coast of Gdańsk Bay itself.

2

The Long Riverside. View from the opposite bank of the river, from the Repository (Szafarnia) where the waters of the New Motława join the Old Motława and divide Granary Island, with the ruins of old granaries, from Lead Island (Ołowianka), not shown on this photograph. In the middle is the Crane, and on the left a line of buildings all the way up to Holy Ghost Gate. In the Crane (see illustration 5) is housed the Central Maritime Museum. This museum occupies the whole building complex which includes the buildings to the right of the Crane. These buildings are a somewhat unsuccessful architectural reference to earlier granary buildings. Three granaries facing the Crane have also been adapted to meet the needs of the Museum - these are on Lead Island (c.f. illustration 4).

3

The Long Riverside seen from the bridge which joins Granary Island to the Main Town and which is also the first part of the road from the Green Gate on the left bank of the Motława to Elbląg. In the compact row of buildings on the Long Riverside can be seen the following gates: Chlebnicka, Mariacka with the house of the Society of Naturalists just before it with its characteristic slender turret, then the Holy Ghost Gate and finally Szeroka Gate with the Crane. In the background we can see the buildings of Lead Island, much changed at the end of the 19th century by the building of the power station there, and part of the wharf on Wartka Street from where photograph 1 was taken. After the destruction of 1945, the Long Riverside was faithfully restored to the shape that had existed for centuries. You could easily imagine that nothing here has changed despite the passing of time, with the one exception that the merchants' counting-houses and the stacks of planks, barrels, goods and ballast-stones have been replaced by souvenir shops and places catering for the needs of the passing tourists. Yet there is something missing, something which defined the character and function of this place for many centuries: the great sea-going ships and their tall masts.

4

Lead Island once belonged to the Teutonic Order as part of the Gdańsk command. The warehouse and workshops located here served as the economic base for the garrison. Three granaries are visible here: Oliwski, fifteenth century but rebuilt in among others 1600, 1677 and 1738, Miedź from the nineteenth century and Panna from the seventeenth century. These granaries were reconstructed with the needs of the Maritime

Museum in mind. The ship moored nearby, the "Sołdek", also belongs to the Museum Complex.

5

The Crane - the symbol of Gdańsk and its character as a port - is joined to the Szeroka Gate in one defensive structure. While it never ceased to play a military role, its main function was as part of the port - loading goods and ballast onto ships and erecting masts. This was a very important function in a crowded port with wharves on both sides of the Motława, Old as well as New, to the south of Granary Island. Ships leaving the port of Gdańsk would pass the Crane and sail past Lead Island on their way to the mouth of the Motława. A gate at the end of Szeroka Street already existed in 1363 and in 1367 we find a Latin reference to a crane: caranum. The Crane gained its present shape in the fifteenth century just after the fire of 1442. Although contemporary with the other water-gates, this one differs from the others considerably, and not simply because of the characteristic massive silhouette of the Crane, built from brick and wood, rising above and dominating the row of buildings on the Long Riverside and leaning over the Motława. The difference lies in the shape of the sides, flanking both the arch of the gate and the Crane itself. They create the impression of circular towers, positioned in such a way and with embrasures so spaced as to give a field of fire over the entire landing-stage and if necessary Granary Island and Lead Island as well. The construction of such a powerful defensive structure, and one placed directly opposite the Teutonic Order's Lead Island, is evidence of the town's growing independence of the feudal Order, or at least a demonstration of the town's growing significance.

6

The Market-Stall Gate (Brama Straganiarska) was constructed in 1482-3, virtually the same time as the Mariacka Gate and it represents the same kind of rectangular building arranged like a crest along the bank of the Motława and enlivened by battlements and flanked by slender turrets. Behind the Gate, in the direction of the Swan Tower which can be seen on the right, stretched the Fishermen's Wharf, and beyond that the elongated irregular shape of the Fish Market. The Swan Tower was not erected until the second half of the XV century. It was the north-east tower in the fortifications encircling the Main Town. It faces the place where the Teutonic Castle once stood. Its construction became possible after 1454 when Teutonic rule ended and the castle was destroyed by Gdańsk burghers at the very beginning of the 13-Year War. The tower which had stood on this spot earlier found itself in the hands of the Order. The new building in the background is the Technical School of Communications. This photograph was taken from the other side of the Motława, from Lead Island, in front of the Maritime Museum granaries and here we can see the bow of the moored museum-ship "Sołdek".

7

This - alongside the Crane - is the second dominant feature of the Long Riverside but its form has incomparably more greatly been rebuilt and dismembered: the Mariacka Gate with the adjoining Naturalists' House on the north-west. The house has its second, main elevation on Mariacka Street (c.f. illustration 60). The small gate closing off Mariacka Steet was built in the second half of the XIV century. In the following century most probably after the end of the war between the Prussian states and Poland and the Teutonic Order, the gate was rebuilt in the shape familiar to other water-gates, notably Chlebnicka and Straganiarska. It is an imposing rectangular building, with many slender niches and numerous windows, and flanked by slender many-sided turrets. Initially the mass of the gate although enlivened by a picturesque chiaroscuro effect caused by the niches, was more unified. The breaking-up of the elevation by the numerous windows is the effect of designating the gate as a place of dwelling in the XVI century, and also because the gate ceased to perform its initial defensive function. The gate's function as a means of communication is not easily discerned - there is only a small archway in the lower part. On the town side of the gate was mounted a gilded stone crest of Gdańsk (see illustration 49), while on the side of the port on the Motława, the crests of Gdańsk, Poland and Royal Prussia. At the end of the XVI century, in 1598, in place of a small old house a town-house was built in the northern mannerist style, one of the biggest and most imposing in Gdańsk. The design, and perhaps even the oversight of the construction, are usually attributed to Anthony van Obberghen, the outstanding town builder and architect, creator of such works as the Old Town Hall (illustration 98) and the Great Armoury (illustration 79, 85). It is known that in the high vaulted cellar flourished a hostelry called the Green Cellar. According to reports from the middle of the XIX century, apparently based on earlier accounts, in this house was based a shoemaker's employing many workers. The upper floors served as warehouse and store-room, while the staircase was located in the corner turret. The picturesque character of this turret was further enhanced in 1866-7 by the addition of a dome on its summit housing an astronomical observatory. The house changed its function in 1845 when it was bought together with the neighbouring Mariacka Gate by the Society of Naturalists, an organisation active in Gdańsk since the XVIII century and with a worthy history in the town. It was as a result of the Society's efforts that the Polytechnic was founded in Gdańsk in 1904. Both buildings housed scientific workshop and a wellstocked library and botanical collection. In its own way a continuation of the character of this building as a place housing a scientific institute and a collection can be seen in the fact that the building is now the premises of the Archaeological Museum, which gained great credit for its researches into the beginnings of Gdańsk (see illustration 60). This photograph was taken from Granary Island opposite the gate.

8

The houses on 11 Długie Pobrzeże on the first floor of which there is the "Gdański Bówka" shop.

9

A view of the Long Riverside from Lead Island, looking south, with the entire frontage of the Main Town along the Motława. All the wide main streets of the town run parallel to each other in the direction of the river (and are only joined to each other by short narrow alley-ways). This shows that the entire life of the town was concentrated on the Motława, on the main route of communication, which crossed here with the second route on land, running through the whole town from the Upland and Golden Gates along Long Street to the Green Gate. The Main Town had seven land gates: 3 each to the south and west, and one to the north, leading to the Old Town and the Castle. Towards the end of the Middle Ages the town had as many as eight water-gates, five of which can be seen on this photograph: Crane, Holy Ghost, Mariacka, Chlebnicka and Green, closing off the Long Market in the place of the Koga Gate. Further along is the Cow Gate at the end of Ogarna Street, originally early Gothic in essence then rebuilt in 1905 in the neo-Romanesque style. The reconstruction after the wartime destruction rather unsuccessfully refers back to the XIX century state (c.f. illustration 99). To the right of the Crane, heading north, are two other gates, already mentioned above: St John's and Straganiarska.

10

The Motława Landing-stage past the bend of the river, near Wartka Street by Zamczysko (the Great Castle). To this point on the Motława stretched the fortifications of the Teutonic Castle, guarding the mouth of the Motława and controlling in this way the entire traffic in the port of Gdańsk. At this wharf are currently moored passenger vessels, ferries and barges. The buildings are modern. Behind a big red town-house is a house in baroque style but with a stepped roof, betraying its gothic origins - here are the premises of the good and well-known Kubicki Restaurant. This restaurant was established by Bolesław Kubicki and was famous before the war not only because of its Polish port character, but also because of its good cuisine and accompanying cabaret.

11

From beyond the Old and New Motława, through the ruins of Granary Island, can be seen the Main Town with its tops and towers dominating the compact town buildings: the Naturalists' House, Mariacka Gate and St Mary's Church.

12

The same stretch of the Long Riverside as in photograph 9. Here we have a view from the Cow Bridge linking Ogarna Street and Granary Island in the opposite northerly direction with the mass of the Green Gate in the foreground. In the most distant background are the buildings of Wartka Street as well as the granaries and the power station on Lead Island. The view is almost from the same place chosen over 200 years ago by Frederick Anthony Lohrmann for his drawing, engraved and published by Matthew Deisch in his album "50 Prospekte von Danzig", in 1765. Deisch came from Augsburg but from 1760 until his death in 1789 he worked in Gdańsk. Lohrmann was from Berlin, but from 1759 to 1773 he lived in Gdańsk then moved to Warsaw where he died in about 1800. On this engraving, reproduced on p. 29, we can clearly see the drawbridge of the Green Bridge as well as a forest of masts on the ships in the port.

13

The Motława Landing-stage looking up-river along Wapiennicka Street and Wartka Street from the place where the Radunia Canal flows into the Motława and where the Motława used to flow into the Vistula before a new channel was dug in 1371 further to the north. The name of Wartka Street ("Lively") comes in fact from the current of the Radunia Canal which was so very different from the slowly flowing waters of the Motława. In the distance we see the compact row of houses by the Fish Market and the Fishermen's Wharf, and further, beyond the Straganiarska Gate, the beginning of the Long Riverside. Above these buildings rise the roofs and towers of St John's Church and further on St Mary's Church, forming as it were the top storey of the town's silhouette. On the left are the buildings of the power station on Lead Island. The first coal-fired power station was built here in 1898, and it was rebuilt in 1899-1913, 1940-1941 and 1959.

14

The Green Gate, southern elevation facing Granary Island. Along here, across the bridge on the Motława, led the land route, through the Stągiewna Gate and further, at the end of Long Gardens, through the mannerist Żuławska Gate, built by Jan Strakowski, on to Żuławy and Elbląg. The most important route, however, followed the seacoast and the Vistula Sand-bar to Sambia and Królewiec, where from ancient times amber, the gold of the north, had come from. It was in this very place, where the ancient trade route joined the via regia (via mercatorum) going from south to north-west, and crossed the water-route, that Gdańsk was founded. The site therefore was chosen with great foresight and judiciousness. To this very day, the land trade route, particularly the section in the town known as the Royal Way, plays a very important role in the life of the Main Town. The eastern end of this route was guarded in the Middle Ages, just after the bestowing of urban rights on the Chełm model, by what seems to be the oldest of the water-gates: the Koga Gate, already being mentioned in 1357 (for comparison, the earliest mention of a gate on Szeroka Street, later the Crane, is dated 1363). The gate took its present form between 1564 and 1568 and was the work of the builder Regnier from Amsterdam, under the supervision of the town architect Jan Kramer from Dresden. The town wanted at the same time to meet its obligation to Kazimierz Jagiellończyk, after the Second Peace of Toruń 1466 and after receiving many royal privileges, to construct in Gdańsk a residence for Polish kings. Fate decreed, however, that although Polish kings stayed many times in Gdańsk, they never stayed in this building, choosing other houses for their seat. The nearest the building came to a royal occupant was when Louise Maria Gonzaga, later the Queen and the wife first of Władysław IV and later of Jan Kazimierz, stayed here when she was passing through from 11 to 20 February 1646. It is worth mentioning that this was the first address of the Naturalists' Society (Sociatas Physica Experimentalis), set up in 1743 by Daniel Gralath, the botanist and physicist, Paul Świetlicki, humanist and linguist, and Matthew Wolff, doctor and astronomer. The Society later moved to the Naturalists' House (c.f. illustration 7). The Gate is an imposing building, protruding beyond the line of the houses to such an extent that the side elevations, called double-axial because they have two windows on each storey, have their own triangular summits. The front elevation is twelve-axial, with three summits: the two outside ones are similar to the sides, while the central one is considerably wider and is raised above the four central axes. The summits are not original but reproductions from 1886. The pilasters which break up the elevation are inserted between pairs of windows, which makes the building better articulated and more rhythmical. On the lower storey four large arches facilitate good communication with the town. The northernmost arch was constructed as late as 1883. The original appearance can be seen in the engraving (reproduced on p. 20) probably made according to the drawing by Peter Willer and published in Reinhold Curicke's "Der Stadt Dantzig historische Beschreibung ..." in 1687. It is difficult to overestimate the significance of this building: it was the first such monumental manifestation of the new style of architecture in Gdańsk - the Renaissance, or rather mannerism in its northern, Dutch style, which would change in such a long-lasting way the gothic face of Gdańsk and give the city its characteristic stamp.

15

One more look at the Long Riverside (from Lead Island) and the serried ranks of the buildings from the Mariacka Gate and the dominating Naturalists' House above it to the Green Gate. The prevailing styles are gothic and mannerism, although we can also see some baroque forms, albeit fairly restrained and almost classical. The whole scene is very picturesque with varied shapes and with the sunlight giving a sharp graphic line to some elevations with their divisions stressing their verticalism and also, besides these, massive compact forms. The whole is crowned with the contours and tracery of the roofs.

16

The centre of the Main Town seen from the south-west with the towers of St Mary's Church and the Town Hall in the distance. In the foreground is one of the two buildings of the so-called Town Court, which was constructed by building onto the south-eastern corner of the medieval defences of the Main Town. The photograph shows a section of the south front and the uppermost parts of the Brewery Tower visible above the ridge of the long building. To the left just out of the photograph are the Schlutz and Corner Towers. The latter, with its adjoining defensive wall, is the oldest element of this complex - its beginnings date back to 1343. Matters connected with the building of the town's fortifications were regulated by the charter of Grand Master Ludolf Konig issued in 1342. From the end of the XIV century and throughout the XV century an additional low external wall was built to improve the defences. The profusion of towers, and the double line of defensive walls to the south and west, are evidence of where the greatest threat lay and of the steps taken to protect this flank. Together with the development of military technology, the erection of modern earthworks and bastions meant that the threat of attack from this side was already being minimalised by the XVI century. It was not by accident that the first modern ramparts and bastions were started in 1547 along the western flank. In the next hundred years, until the 1660s, Gdańsk was encircled by a mighty ring of fortifications, first in Italian style, then Dutch, making the town into an invincible fortress (c.f. illustration 9 on p. 15). From this time also the significance of the medieval walls began to decline and their material began to be used for various building purposes. Between 1616 amd 1619 the town builder Jan Strakowski built the Town Court between the walls on the site of earlier buildings. The Court housed the stables, the coach-houses and the mint. In front of the building between the walls and between the Main Town and the Old Suburb, an imposing wooden building was constructed at the beginning of the XVII century. This was the Fencing School but it was not only used for the practice of swordsmanship but also for the performance of theatrical productions. There was an open-air stage as well as covered galleries for the public. The vibrant theatrical atmosphere is testified to by the frequent apearances on this stage of English actors with their Shakespearean repertoire in the first half of the XVII century. Also many perfomances could be heard in German, Latin, and even Polish. The Royal Court Opera from Warsaw also appeared here during the visit to Gdańsk of Queen Louise Maria in 1646. The type and character of this building and its condition in the third quarter of the XVII century can be seen on the engraving by Piotr Willer, published in Reinhold Curicke's chronicle of Gdańsk and reproduced on p. 30. It is worth adding that between 1885 and 1887 an imposing brick synagogue, which was taken down in 1939, was built in this place. As a result of the destruction which took place in 1945 the whole complex of buildings was turned to rubble. Only the Corner Tower and a small section of the walls survived. During the reconstruction not only the Town Court and the Brewery Tower but also the Schlutz Tower, which had been destroyed in 1846, were rebuilt. The Schlutz Tower was named in honour of Jan Karl Schlutz, the Gdańsk draughtsman and graphic artist, professor and rector of the School of Fine Arts, who had unsuccessfully campaigned against the destruction of the Tower.

17

The Green Gate seen this time from inside the town from one of the antethresholds on the south side of Długi Targ (The Long Market). The Gate closes off this narrow elongated space, directing the attention and the thoughts of all Gdańsk's citizens away from the land, away from the south and the west, to the Motława, to the water, to Gdańsk's window onto the whole world. This is where the trade route inside the town ends, leading as it does from the west and the south further to the east. At the same time, having passed all the gates and all the most important public buildings, this is where the Royal Way ends. This square, The Long Market, would lose on holidays its mercantile character: here would take place all the town ceremonies, and here also in beautiful surroundings would the arrival of splendid guests be celebrated.

18

The same square - The Long Market - seen from the other side, underneath one of the arches of the Green Gate, in the direction of the slender shape of the Town Hall which closes off the square at the western end. The Main Town Hall is situated at the corner of The Long Market, and its longer side is on Long Street (ulica Długa), the town's main communication artery (c.f. illustration 4 on p. 10, a reproduction from Curicke's Chronicle). In 1379-1382, just after the renewal of the foundation charter, the modest older building was replaced by a new two-storey building. The charter, issued on July 5, 1378 by Grand Master Winrych von Kniprode confirmed and broadened the Main Town's rights to self-government. It was not a coincidence that the year 1379 also saw the rebuilding of the Parish Church of the Blessed Virgin Mary. Both of these projects were connected with the builder Henry Ungeradin (c.f. commentary to illustration 45). Later the Town Hall was constantly being rebuilt and beautified, as befitted the growing needs of the town's administration and jurisdiction, and commensurate with the growing power and representative needs of the Town Council. The building of the tower was commenced in 1465, after the removal of the Teutonic Order from the town. During the next phase of rebuilding in 1486-1492 the building was given its final shape, gaining an extra storey and a tall attic roof from the Long Market side. At the same time the tower was built up to its present height and was given its tapering spire which, however, was replaced sixty years later by one even taller in the then-popular renaissance-mannerist style. It survived in this form until 1945 and in this form was rebuilt. (c.f. illutration 35). This is not the end of the story. Between 1593 and 1596 a new section, not visible on this photograph, consisting of three wings around a small courtyard, was added on the northern side in order to increase the internal dimensions of the Town Hall which was constantly proving too small. Finally the town builder Anthony van Obberghen designed new and bigger windows in stone surrounds at the very end of the XVI century. Not much has survived from the original very rich interior furniture and fittings (c.f. the interior of the Kamlaria on the second floor of the Town Hall, immortalised in the middle of the XIX century by Jan Karol Schlutz, illustration 12, p. 18). A fortunate survivor is the Red Hall (Sala Czerwona), the Great Council Chamber, one of the most beautiful mannerist interiors, the work of Gdańsk and Dutch artists from 1593 to 1598: Jan Vredeman de Vries, Willem van der Meer and Szymon Hoerle. The ceiling paintings were completed in 1608 by Isaac van den Blocke, son of the sculptor Willem from Mechelen, but resident in Gdańsk, and brother of the sculptor and architect Abraham.

19

Artus Court. After the granting of urban rights on the Chełm model in 1342-1346, in place of the previously binding Lubeck model, during further rebuilding of the town, in the central position by the Town Hall on the north side of The Long Market, a plot was allocated for Artus Court. The fact that "curia regis Artura" is already being mentioned in 1350 shows how quickly the work must have progressed. Artus Courts were also known in many other Baltic towns, particularly in places occupied by the Teutonic Order. None of the other courts, however, either those still existing or those known from iconographic records, achieved such excellent artistic form. These courts were the seats of brotherhoods, whose members were recruited from the wealthiest merchant and patrician classes. These brotherhoods, a form of exclusive association, patterned themselves on the legend of King Arthur and the Knights of the Round Table, stressing the democratic character thereof, the equality of its members, but also nurturing the ideals of chivalry, both in terms of social customs and in bravery and the perfection of fighting ability. Obviously the town had to defend itself; even though all adult citizens were obliged to take up arms in times of need, the richest strata used this means to raise their own prestige and pride. The first brick building of the Court was constructed in 1380 and was considerably smaller and humbler than the present one, but it was reserved exclusively for only one, in fact the oldest, brotherhood of merchants - the Brotherhood of St. George. After the fire of 1476, the present construction was built in 1481. In the spacious hall of the new Court, under star-covered vaulting supported on four slender granite pillars, seven brotherhoods had their seats, called benches. They all competed with one another in the decoration of the interior (c.f. Schlutz's engraving from 1848 on p. 12). In the face of such competition, and also as a result of the admission of lower classes to the Court, i.e. the common craftsmen and tradesmen, the most exclusive knightly brotherhood of St. George began a few years later to build its own new seat (see illustration 87 and engraving 10 on p. 16). The facade of Arthur's Court, although rebuilt on two later occasions, has retained its three enormous pointed-arch windows, which allow a great amount of daylight into the interior, The extremely interesting and picturesque rear elevation, usually so very much more modest than the front, gives an indication of how rich must have been the decoration of this late gothic Court and in particular its summit. The renaissance reconstruction from 1552 with the arcaded loggia above these large windows was carried out to commemorate the visit of Zygmunt August and betrays Italian influences. Two paintings of this building can be seen in the Main Town Hall: "Grosz Czynszowy" ("Penny rent") by Anton Moeller in 1601 and "The Apotheosis of Gdańsk" by Isaac van den Blocke from 1608. The elevation received its present shape in 1616-1617 and is the work of Abraham van den Blocke, the architect and sculptor, and member of the artistic family which had such an important influence on the shaping of the mannerist style in Gdańsk and the further spreading of this style not only throughout Pomerania (Royal Prussia) but also in the rest of Poland. The subject matter of the sculptures on the facade reflect the public and representational function of the Court. The four figures between the windows represent: Scipio Africanus, Themistocles, Marcus Furius Camillus and Judas Macchabeus, figures well known from Jewish, Greek and Roman history, symbolising civic virtues and love of one's country. Their complements are the statues in the attic of the summit, personifying Justice and Strength (Iustitia and Fortitudo), with Fortune on the coping. The line of the lintel is broken by the entrance to the wine-cellar which was established in 1651 in neo-classical form and whose right door-jamb can be seen on photograph 21. Official receptions, theatrical performances, brotherhood meetings, revels, and later also trade transactions - these were the basic functions of the Court. At the same time as the facade of the Court received its final appearance, so the Neptune Fountain was given its final shape. This fountain is both extremely popular and extremely successful in forming the architectural climate of The Long Market (photographs 24, 27-28). On both sides of Artus Court are town-houses which at various times served as the seat of the Court of Assessors. On the left is the Old Bench-house which functioned from 1549 to 1713, and on the right is the New Bench-house, 1713-1806 (see photograph 23), also known as the Gdańsk Vestibule (Sień Gdańska) as it was mostly here in the great hallway of this town-house that the great collections of Gdańsk art from the collection of the merchant Lesser Giełdziński were exhibited from 1901.

20

Medieval plots of land, although quite often long, were as a rule narrow. In modern times many of these slender gothic town-houses had no more than a fashionable face-lift and a change of roof-style. It sometimes happened, however, that in place of two of these houses an imposing and richly decorated and furnished house would be built like the one at 20 The Long Market. The proportions, the way of dividing up the facade, the interior function layout - all of these follow a certain deeply - rooted pattern, adapted equally to the character and the needs of the inhabitants. Ornament, or the so-called great order - the division of the elevation with the help of pilasters running up through several storeys and not just one - all of this is an indication of the baroque features of this building, rebuilt in 1680. The style and the high quality of the plastic decoration lead us to ascribe the work to Andrzej Schluter the younger. The house on the right - number 19 - is the Hotel Jantar, formerly the Hotel du Nord, built in 1842. Jan Matejko was a guest here in 1877 during his journey through Pomerania to Prussia to the field of Grunwald (Tannenberg) at the time of painting his "Battle of Grunwald". The hotel was rebuilt once again in 1905 and gained its present appearance during the reconstruction after the Second World War.

21-22

The wide steps leading up to Artus Court were decorated with a pair of stone lions - the characteristic supporters of Gdańsk's coat of arms. It must be admitted that they look good here both from the artistic and from the ideological point of view but they are here by chance. The original place for which they were destined was the Gate of St. James completed in 1633 on the north side of the Old Town by Jan Strakowski. He was responsible also for the other gates: Brama Nizinna (Lowland Gate) on the north side of the Old Suburb, and Brama Żuławska (Żuławy Gate) on the road heading east to Elbląg. This gate was adapted to suit the new type of earthworks and bastions at a time when the number of roads leaving Gdańsk was limited. The beautiful portal of Artus Court, the work of Abraham van den Blocke, includes a medallion depicting two kings: Zygmunt III and Władysław IV. It is only when you enter the Court that you can understand the meaning of the decoration of the facades: Fortune is protecting the town which is both strong and just and is upheld by the virtues of its citizens which have derived from ancient prototypes. Every modern manifestation of these exemplars finds itself, just like the whole town, under the vigilant protection of the two kings.

23

A fragment of the northern side of The Long Market, between Artus Court and Furrier's Street (ulica Kuśnierska). On several occasions - in 1587, 1593, 1594 and 1598 - these town-houses served as the temporary residence of King Zygmunt III Waza. From left to right, with numbers going down from 43 to 39, we have the following houses: the New Bench-house, or Gdańsk Vestibule (c.f. illustration 19), a baroque town-house from the end of the XVII century with a portal dated 1567 which is undoubtedly authentic but which was transferred here from another plot; occupying the central position in this group the Golden House (Złota Kamienica), of which more later; next a house with a narrow reconstructed facade from about 1580; finally, an imposing house on the corner of Furrier's Street in the baroque style of about 1700. Initially there were three plots in this place but they were joined together and the architect Jan Kramer built a house for the minter Kasper Goebel. From 1658 this building housed the Royal Post Office. The Gold House stands in the place occupied previously by a gothic building, whose owner at the beginning of the XV century was Arnold Hecht, mayor of Gdańsk. He was executed together with a second mayor, Konrad Leczkow, and his son-in-law, councillor Bartłomiej Gross, in 1411 on the orders of the Teutonic Commander Henryk von Plauen as a reprisal against the town for its insubordination to the Order after the Battle of Grunwald. The initiator of the mannerist reconstruction was Jan Speimann, who held at the beginning of the XVII century the highest offices and honours in the town: in 1601 he was a member of the Bench, then two years later he became a councillor , and finally in 1613 mayor. The house takes its second name - Speimann House - from him. From 1768 to 1918 the owners were the Steffens family, and the house takes yet another of its names from them. The Gold House, or at least its facade, was designed and built by Abraham van den Blocke, while the rich gilded artistic decoration comes from the years 1616-1618 and is the work of his collaborator, the sculptor Jan Vogt from Rostock. The date 1609 carved on the balustrade which crowns the building could therefore either indicate the beginning of construction or its completion. The Gold House is one of the foremost monuments in Gdańsk, and not only because of the wealth of materials, the richness and high artistic quality of the decorations of the facade. It must be emphasised that despite the huge amount of destruction most of its elements are authentic (c.f. illustration 25-26). The exceptional value of this town-house lies also in the fact that it serves as a model which enables us to understand the essence and character of a modern patrician Gdańsk town-house. The slender facade and the vertical rhythms of the windows recall the design of gothic elevations, with the exception that instead of shaped pillars by the wall, creating niches, here we have pilasters. The partitioning of the facade by the hierarchy of orders (the so-called layering of orders, from the bottom up: Doric, Ionic, Corinthian, and hermas in the attic wall covering the sloping summit), and the emphasising of the horizontal divisions, are a clear reference to the classical tradition, to the style of the Italian renaissance. On the other hand, the method of applying these divisions, the introduction of large rectangular windows with a densely-barred frame, the wealth of decoration giving the wall an artistic and ornamental articulacy at the expense of the legibility of the tectonic divisions, indicates a link with the northern European, Dutch variety of mannerism. Traditional functionalism from the Middle Ages, renaissance motifs drawn from antiquity, mannerism in its northern version - these are three basic elements constituting the character and appearance of the middle-class town-house in Gdańsk at the end of the XVI century and in the first half of the XVII century, the time of the town's great flowering from which comes the majority of buildings of a domestic nature in the Main Town either which have survived or which were rebuilt after the Second World War. At the same time, all of these features: slender facades, the rhythm of the windows, the architectual and artistic frame, the chiaroscuro effect and the lively decoration. all have their clear counterparts in the architecture of the Netherlands, particularly of Antwerp.

24

T he building of the Royal Post Office, 39 The Long Market, seen from beyond the Neptune Fountain (see photograph 27).

25-26

T wo fragments of the facade of the Gold House, giving an indication of the rich meaning of this artistic decoration. The unusually flamboyant iconographic programme could not have come into existence without the participation of Jan Speimann himself. In his person were combined the enterprising merchant and administrator with the humanist and engineer of wide interests. This decoration is made up of both typical and unique elements, the latter of which are quite astounding. There are precisely sculpted reliefs of battle-scenes with many figures on the friezes between storeys and between these the busts of individual figures on the partitioned axes of the pilasters. These are people and events from ancient history - Greek, Jewish, but primarily Roman (Judas Macchabeus, Themistocles, Mucius Scaevola, Camilius, Scipio Africanus, Brutus and the assassination of Caesar, Horatius), and also from European and contemporary history - the Emperor Henry, the Polish Kings Kazimierz Jagiellończyk and Zygmunt III Waza, or on one of the reliefs: the battle between the Hungarian leader Huniady and Skandenberg, the Albanian national hero, from the XV century. The whole effect is completed by four full figures on the balustrade of the attic, in various poses and with various gestures. Depicted here are figures from ancient history, mythology or literature: Cleopatra, Oedipus, Achilles, Antigone. The entrance to the Gold House is guarded by the personifications of three theological virtues: Christian love (Caritas) is the figure over the portal, while Faith (Fides) and Hope (Spes) are in reliefs above the archway. The design is completed by the panoply on the pilasters (elements of arms and armour in decorative festoons). The House, therefore, is guarded by virtue and valour.

27

T he Neptune Fountain: the idea of locating a fountain in front of Artus Court is almost contemporary with the renaissance reconstruction of 1552, of which nothing now remains. The Fountain was erected in 1549, only to be replaced at the beginning of the XVII century by the present one, a few years before the rebuilding of the facade of the Court, and in strict keeping with it, in order to create the most harmonious artistic and architectural form of the most important square in Gdańsk. The design of the fountain is ascribed to Abraham van den Blocke, who was responsible not only for the details but also for its spatial relationship to the square, the communication routes, the views and the most important buildings. His workshop also realised between 1604 and 1613 the stone elements of the base and the surrounds. The figure of the god of the sea was cast in bronze by the sculptor Piotr Husen in Gert Benningk's workshop, the biggest foundry in Gdańsk. It is not known whether Husen himself, well known for his work in Copenhagen, was the designer of the sculpture. Attempts to find artists from southern Germany failed, as did the journey of Abraham van den Blocke to Augsburg, one of the centres of casting, in 1619.

The figure itself may well have aroused feelings of dissatisfaction among members of the Town Council, who had commissioned the statue, and certainly in Jan Speimann, the mayor at that time, and one of the main initiators of the undertaking, an educated man with refined artistic tastes. The figure's over-heavy form may be explained by the need to fit it into the large space of the square. The statue did not realise the mannerist demand of having such an appearance from every side that it should bring a new compositional formulation, with dynamic new form, line and direction; if it had complied with this stylistic demand from every side, it would be equally beautiful everywhere. The statue presents itself most successfully from the sides (admittedly very important, because this is along the main communication axis of Long Street and The Long Market !) and from the front and side, particularly on the south-west, i.e. the corner of Ławnicza Street, as on the photograph, The view from directly in front is less successful, and worst of all is the rear view, the one which would have been seen by all the notables as they came out of Artus Court. To be fair to the sculptor, however, (he was not after all an educated artist or one used to working in the best sculpting environments in Europe at that time), he managed, or at least wanted, to compose the statue according to the fashionable rule of style, and furthermore, also in keeping with mannerist norms, composed it from worthy and respected patterns, as well as elaborating it by copying three different fragments of ancient statues. The treatment of the head with the curly hair and of the torso with the marked musculature, specially designed for the rays of the sun to deepen every furrow, clearly betray the statue's ancient origins. The double twist of the body on the other hand belongs to the mannerist school of human figures. The work was finally completed and installed many years later, after the deaths of Speimann and van den Blocke. This was done in 1633 by the latter's pupil and collaborator, Wilhelm Richter, who married his master's widow and took over his workshop. At this time Jan Rogge constructed the ironwork. The gates were crowned with the crests of Poland and of Gdańsk in the middle of the XVIII century when the Fountain was completely refurbished. At the same time, from 1757 to 1761, the sculptor Jan Stender created a new stem for the base and a new surround for the basin together with sculptures of fantastic animals and sea creatures, all in the rococo style fashionable at the time. The Fountain was partly dismantled and survived the war quite well - only the stem suffered badly and had to be reconstructed. Because of the skilful stone-work realising the design of the well-known sculptor Tadeusz Godziszewski, and also because of the action of water over the years, it would be difficult to find any dissonance between the original and reconstructed parts. The basic source of the flow of water is the trident held by the lord of the seas and oceans in his right hand, as well as the sea-horses at his feet and the edge of the pedestal. The water falls into the bowl of the fountain and from there in powerful streams spewed out by the gargoyles down to the lower basin.

28

The crests of Poland and Gdańsk on the tops of the four gates leading to the area around the fountain were added during the renovations in the XVIII century and were the work of iron-worker Jan Baren. In 1935 the eagles were broken off by the Hitler Youth. They were reconstructed after the war.

29

An unusually characteristic element of Gdańsk town-houses, and indeed of the whole appearance of the streets, is the antethreshold. The beginnings were prosaic: it was a question of dividing the direct entrance from the street to the cellar from the actual entrance to the part of the building designed for dwelling, trade or craft. It was also significant that the ground floor was often very high because of the proximity of the water and the damp terrain. With time these ante-thresholds were reconstructed, with effective stair arrangements, richly decorated balustrades and pillars forming a representative framework for the main entrance. There was also a terrace which was used on days with good weather as a place of rest, entertainment or social meetings. The Gdańsk antethresholds, mostly built during the XIX century, created problems for communications in the narrow streets and for the establishment of modern shops. Most of them were destroyed in 1945 and were reconstructed in order to recreate the characteristic climate of the town on the most important streets: Mariacka Street and The Long Market, as well as partly on Piwna Street, Holy Ghost Street and to a lesser degree on Ogarna Street. The ante-thresholds shown on the photograph are from a few town-houses on the south side of The Long Market, from number 11 to number 14 and are mostly reconstructions (among others based on those from Long Street and Piwna Street) using many of the original preserved elements. The photograph serves as an illustration of the methods and character of the work of the restorers during the hugescale rebuilding of the old centre of Gdańsk. All of the fragments which had survived from given town-houses were gathered together and others, consistent with function and style and equally authentic, were accumulated from other places and buildings and completed with new parts and elements modelled on original patterns. As a result, a whole was created which was not entirely authentic but which faithfully recreated the character and climate of Gdańsk's streets and town-houses. The inaccuracy and infidelity of the compilation is recompensed by the unrepeatable atmosphere of these nooks and crannies.

30

𝕿 wo rococo portals of two neighbouring town-houses on The Long Market, numbers 5 and 6. The skill of the renovators and the stone-workers, together with the patina of dozens of years, make it difficult to believe that this is a fairly free reconstruction: the right portal is patterned on the late rococo portal of the town-house at 14 Long Street from 1777, while the left portal successfully refers to XVIII century forms but is in fact the work of the stone-workers engaged in the great rebuilding of Gdańsk's historical monuments.

31

𝕿 he Panorama of Gdańsk at the top of the triumphal arch - at the top of the painting is the Apotheosis of Gdańsk (also called the Allegory of Gdańsk Trade, or the Allegory of the Union of Gdańsk with Poland, both of which titles seriously limit the ideological scope of the painting). This large oval painting is in the very centre of the ceiling in the Red Hall (Sala Czerwona) of the Main Town Hall and was painted in 1608 by Isaac van den Blocke. The town of Gdańsk occupies a central position in this painting between the earthly kingdom, the Crown of the Kingdom of Poland, and the heavenly kingdom. It links the two kingdoms and draws from both its prosperity and welfare. Above everything, however, rules Providence: from the clouds, on which can be seen the Hebrew letters IHWH, comes a hand wielding the lofty tower of the Town Hall, as a symbol of the Town and the Council, the town community and the parish faithful alike, all witnessing to God's protection, to the fact that this civitas has been chosen by God, and that its welfare is a result of this choice - we can clearly detect here echoes of Calvin's theory of predestination. The inscription which has been placed on both sides of the hand reads: ISTA SERVAT SUB HIS ALIS and the wings by the tower indicate that this town finds itself under the protection of God's wings. The silhouette of the town, although a faithful picture of the western panorama, was also shown with a symbolic meaning in mind: in the centre are three buildings clearly emphasised and elevated above the others: the Town Hall, St. Mary's Church and the Upland Gate. Although Providence's hand is upon the Town Hall, Providence and the inscription Jehovah are above the very centre - and here is St. Mary's Church with its tall massive tower. This fortress, this town of God, is surrounded by fortified ramparts beyond which other public and sacred buildings rise, but in such a way that the whole silhouette of the town seems to be falling away to the sides. The only entrance to the town leads through the Upland Gate, positioned exactly in the middle and above which is the Prison Tower. The Gate gives the possibility of entry to the town but it also guards the town like a compact, sealed organism, totally subject to the will of God.

32

The town-houses on the south side of The Long Market (numbers 1-4) opposite Arthur's Court, served as royal quarters in the XVII and XVIII centuries to meet the needs of Polish kings temporarily in Gdańsk: Zygmunt III, Władysław IV, Jan Kazimierz, Jan III, August II of Saxony and Stanisław Leszczyński. It was here, in the house at number 2, that Queen Marysieńka, wife of Jan III Sobieski, during the six-month stay of the couple in Gdańsk, gave birth to their son Alexander on 9 September. The first of these town-houses was restored in the classical style of about 1800, the second in the mannerist style of the first half of the XVII century, the third, with the great order on the facade, betrays baroque features from the third quarter of the XVII century and is ascribed to Andrzej Schluter the younger. The antethreshold of house number 1 comes from Piwna Street, the decorated stone reliefs of numbers 2 and 3 are partly authentic. Particularly valuable is the post from 1577 flanking the stairs to number 2 - this is one of the oldest surviving antethreshold posts in Gdańsk.

33

The main entrance to the Town Hall: against the background of the plain south wall, enlivened only by windows whose varicty and rhythm betray the many stages of building (c.f. commentary to photograph 18), the entrance stands out because of its monumental artistic sculptural-architectural form.
The double flight of stairs, bordered by a stone balustrade adds more elegance. The portal, supported on two Corinthian columns, above the archway of the main entrance, includes a huge relief of the crest of Gdańsk, traditionally in the company of two lions who are holding the crest, with the exception that the one on the left is not looking at the coat of arms but in the direction of the end of Long Street, at the Golden Gate. According to legend the lion is longingly looking out for the Polish king whose royal procession would enter from this direction. This is supposed to represent the growing longing of the Council and the town, the desire for an improvement in the situation in the light of the increasing threat from the Kingdom of Prussia. The portal is the work of Daniel Eggert from 1766 to 1768, significantly only a few years before the First Partition of Poland.

34

The southern summit of the Town Hall with the high attic wall and with the characteristic forms of late-gothic Flemish architecture: the wall, flanked by two slender octagonal turrets, is divided by windows, blind windows and above all by deep, sharply-pointed niches on the entire height of the wall. The sunlight emphasises the smooth surfaces, the sharp contours and the solid mass, aided by the cornice mouldings and the richly-shaped niches, where the shadows fall most expressively. This wall was built between 1486 and 1492, and was crowned in 1562 with a stone balustrade on which were carved the crests of the Kingdom of Prussia, Poland and Gdańsk, at the same time as the turrets gained their azure renaissance-mannerist cupolas. This photograph was taken from in front of the entrance to Artus Court, with the figure of Mercury, god of trade and commerce, seen against the background of the summit of the Town Hall. This figure was based on the well-known sculpture by Giovanni Battista da Bologna, known as Giambologna, and symobolised Gdańsk's enterprise and trade, as well as the wealth and significance of the town. The figure was placed here in the second half of the XIX century near the entrance leading to the wine-vault in the cellars of the Court (c.f. photograph 19).

35

The cupola on the tower of the Main Town Hall: this tall cupola has many levels and is in the rich renaissance-mannerist style. It was built after the fire of 1556 by Dirk Daniels from Zealand. On completion of the work in 1561 the cupola was crowned with the figure of King Zygmunt August. At the same time Jan Moor s'Hertogenbosch from northern Brabant placed a carillion in the cupola - a set of bells playing melodies.

36

Kaletnicza Street (Purse-makers), running from Long Street towards St. Mary's Church whose massive tower closes off the view of the street.

37

The portal of Uphagen's House at 12 Long Street. In the place of an earlier baroque town-house, the councillor Jan Uphagen, owner of this property from 1775, commissioned a year later Jan Benjamin Dreyer to build a new house in rococo-early classical style. Uphagen tastefully furnished his house with furniture and other fittings, and made a will before his death in 1802 stipulating that his house be left as it was, giving a picture of the luxurious life and culture of a Gdańsk patrician at the end of the XVIII century. The house survived in this state, as a kind of museum open to the public, until the last war. It was rebuilt respecting the original layout of the interior, together with the great vestibule on the ground floor. The facade is a complete reconstruction, while the portal is authentic with the exception of the ironwork of the transom window and the wooden doors, painstakingly recreated by the restorers.

38

Above the compact and tightly-packed domestic buildings can be seen more significant buildings majestically dominating the town. Dom Anielski (The Angel's House) on the left (see photograph 43), crowned with a slender turret, is an exception here. As a rule the taller buildings are public or church edifices, such as for example the huge mass of St Mary's Basilica. This is how Gdańsk must have appeared to travellers coming by land from the east from afar - the view was made possible by the flat landscape of the Żuławy region, all the way up to the Stągiewna Gate (c.f. photograph 102).

39-40

The portal and summit of the town-house at 35 Long Street, known as "The Lion's Castle". The house was built in 1569, probably by Jan Kramer, and represents the short period of domination of renaissance-classical architecture, before the great fascination with the art and decoration of Dutch mannerism. It is an imposing building of noble proportions, with divided pilasters whose articulation and form are consistent with the Italian theory of architecture. There is no profusion of decoration here - only in the friezes between storeys and on the summit. This is the work of the Dutch sculptor Frederick Vroom from Haarlem. It would be hard to find in Gdańsk a better juxtaposition of these two worlds: northern-European sensitivity expressing itself through rich decoration and crossing of accepted boundaries, in an architectural composition caught here in the strict framework of the classical character. The portal, destroyed in 1945, was reconstructed from fragments rescued from the rubble: an example of the uncommon care taken in salvaging them, and in the painstaking arrangement of them into a recreated whole. Schlutz's engraving from 1854 reproduced on p. 19 shows the Great Vestibule of this town-house, as beautifully and elegantly arranged as the facade. The Great Vestibule, two storeys high, was the most representational interior of all Gdańsk town-houses. We can see here the characteristic large cupboards, on which were arranged Chinese vases, or more usually Dutch faience imitations of them from Delft. The vestibule occupied the whole depth of the first building and was separated from the rooms in the back and from the entrance to the outbuildings and to the courtyard by an arcaded wall, behind which were the stairs leading to the upper storeys. This interior did not survive the catastrophe of 1945 either. At the beginning of the XV century the owner of the house standing on this plot was the councillor Bartłomiej Gross, executed in 1411 (see commentary to photograph 23).

41

Chlebnicka Street (Bakers' Street) - a fragment of the southern side in the direction of the Motława, beginning from Number 11, where on the plain brick facade we can see the restored mannerist portal with Tuscan columns. At number 14 we can see a reconstructed late-gothic house (c.f. illustration 42), while in the background this row of town-houses is completed by The Angel's House (photograph 42). These town-houses, after their post-war destruction and reconstruction, were designated as a hostel for students from the Fine Arts Academy and the Music Academy.

42

The house with gothic features at 14 Chlebnicka Street, near the English House, is quite a singular place. From about 1520 until 1822 on this spot stood a late-gothic town-house, standing out against the background of brick-built Gdańsk houses because of its stone-clad facade. The portal and the tracery around the windows of the lower storeys were particularly rich in shape. This house was particularly admired by Prince Wilhelm, later Kaiser Wilhelm I, at whose request the house was bought, dismantled and carefully rebuilt on Peacock Island in Potsdam by Karl Friedrich Schinkel in 1827 as part of the so-called Gdańsk House. The current reconstruction was completed quite recently, after over 150 years of wandering. The view is of the front of the house from Grząska Street (Muddy Street).

43

The Angel's House (or English House) is the second surviving middle-class house built by Jan Kramer. Soon after the completion of the Lion's Castle (photograph 39-40), or perhaps even at the same time, this architect from Dresden built an imposing house completed in 1570 for the merchant Dirck Lylge van Werlen from Westphalia. It was in fact a town palace, the tallest and most spacious of the contemporary middle-class houses, built on two plots of land, six-axial on its main storeys, with a vestibule almost double the normal height on the ground floor, with three main storeys and a three-storey summit, which, very unusually, was repeated above the side and rear elevations. Above the summits rises a slender turret (c.f. photograph 38). The name of the house comes from the figure of the angel crowning the summit of the facade on Chlebnicka Street. The arcaded portal is shaped like a triumphal arch while the whole facade is carefully divided by vertical and horizontal elements: prominent cornice mouldings between the windows are further emphasised by wide friezes; pairs of windows are separated by doubled pilasters. The plainness of this framework has been softened by original black and white sgraffiti, covering the whole of the free surface of the walls, and by gilded and black and red polychroming on the mouldings and friezes. Certain Dutch influences can be seen above all in the shapes of the summit edges and in the use of big windows with stone surrounds and small panes of glass. This does not diminish, however, the impression of firm links with Saxon architecture, which was given to the town by years of Jan Kramer's work, from 1565 to 1577. Two years after finishing the house Dirck Lylge went bankrupt. Clearly, despite his wealth, the construction and maintenance of such an impressive seat, in effect a magnate's town palace, was beyond his means. The often-used name, the English House, comes from the fact that between 1640 and 1687 part of this house was leased by English merchants as a cloth store. The house saw many changes of fortune: at the beginning of the XIX century it became a hotel, while in this century a counting-house for private enterprise. Between 1914 and 1921 it was the seat of the masonic lodge "Chain over the Vistula". At one time the building housed the British Chapel. After the destruction of WW II, restoration work was concluded in 1980.

44

The tower of St. Mary's Church, the same as on photograph 36, seen from the northern side, from the distance beyond the Dominican Church of St. Nicholas, whose eastern summit of the presbyterium is visible on the photograph. Here we have a view of several streets: Szewska (Shoe-makers'), Złotników (Goldsmiths'), Szklarzy (Glaziers'), and Lawendowej (Lavender), which perpendicularly cut across the organism of the Main Town.

45

St. Mary's Church, proudly rising above the town buildings and rivalled only by the Town Hall tower, from where this photograph was taken. This is the main church of Gdańsk, the church of the Council, and here it is seen in all its glory, with its massive shape relieved by its summits and corner turrets, and lightened by its large windows. The great nave of the church rises above the town. The size of this church is indeed impressive and inside it is emphasised by the length and width of its seemingly never-ending naves and aisles, so brightly lit. This church was not always so big. Building commenced in 1343, the year that peace was established between the Teutonic Order and King Kazimierz the Great, a peace that introduced political and economic stability, and during the process of conferring the town urban rights on the Chełm model between 1342 and 1346. The charter of Grand Master Rudolf König in 1342 established property rights in the town and it also affected the plot of land for the Church of the Blessed Virgin Mary as well as the building of the town's fortifications. A second document, issued by Henryk Dusemar on 31 VII 1346 removed the last vestiges of the Lubeck charter and became the legal basis for the acquisition of goods as well as for legal procedures. The church was built of quite modest size as a basilica, which continued in a way the chain of brick-built parish basilicas in the Baltic sea-coast Hanseatic towns. It was not by accident that in 1379, one fear after the ratification and broadening of the Chełm charter by Winrych von Kniprode on 5 VII 1378, which resulted in increased independence of feudal domination by the Teutonic Order (this document also included decisions as to the payments to the church), the unfinished building work was halted. A contract was signed with the master builder Henry Ungeradin which completely changed the shape of the shrine and in so doing greatly increased the internal dimensions. As the result of work which continued until 1502, a huge church arose with a nave and two aisles, also with a three-part presbyterium and transept (on the northern side one of the transept aisles is missing because of the existing buildings of the presbytery) - a huge area which allowed the whole of town society to assembly here, in the spirit of middle-class democracy. How far this building is from the mystical saturation of coloured light from the soaring interior of a gothic cathedral directed towards the main altar and leading the faithful irresistibly in that direction. Here there is a calm space with the rhythm of rows of pillars closed off by way of contrast by crystal vaulting, uncommonly rich in decoration and chiaroscuro effect, with great variety of design, different in every bay. Also on the outside the gothic elements are missing - no loftiness, no ascending, no tearing away of the whole structure from the earth, no upward movement. Here is a mass with plain walls, in which have been cut huge openings for windows; the unadorned walls contrast with the decorated summits and the delicate turrets. There is contrast between the horizontal mass of the building and the slender vertical elements, and between the static mass and the vibrant decoration. Besides all this there is the majesty of unaffected calm.

46

One of Gdańsk's most picturesque corners, faithfully re-enacting the medieval atmosphere of the town organism: the corner of Podkramarska Street (Stallholders' Street) coming at right angles to the northern transept of St Mary's Church and Plebania Street (Presbytery Street), winding its way around the presbytery buildings of the church seen on the left and the mass of the transept and the presbyterium. Before dawn we can already see the town-houses on Mariacka Street. Apart from old engravings or archive photographs, this is the only indication we have of the crowded buildings sealing off the Basilica of St. Mary. The church would appear slowly from the surrounding buildings in the pre-dawn light, revealing itself in fragments only, before showing itself in its full majesty.

47

Presbytery Street is a small alley-way between the presbytery buildings and the Church of St. Mary's. The reconstruction of the medieval complex of parish buildings was undertaken by the then parish priest and later Bishop of Warmia Maurycy Ferber, from the outstanding patrician family. The stone portal from 1518 and the shield with the Ferber coat of arms - three boars' heads - indicate the founder and the date of completion of the building. The gothic-renaissance style of the portal denotes the time of change from the Middle Ages to the modern in the history and culture of Gdańsk. The coping of the portal, with its baroque festoons, is the result of rebuilding in 1715.

48

Mariacka Street - today the most enchanting of Gdańsk's streets, with completely reconstructed antethresholds, splendidly recreates the unrepeatable climate and character of the old buildings in the Main Town. This used to be one of the more modest streets in Gdańsk, away from the main communication and trade routes, between the eastern elevation of St. Mary's Church and the Long Riverside on the Motława. The houses here were never very impressive or rich, they were not as tastefully furnished, and the best artists and the greatest means passed them by. In particular, the modernisation of the town in the XIX and XX centuries left the street unchanged. This all meant that this small street could be fully restored. If you are passing by and are not in a hurry, if you like to please your eye with sights which are beautiful and full of grace and charm, if you like to immerse yourself in history amidst the bustle of modern life, then this is the place to which to come.

49

The previous photograph with the view of Mariacka Street looking west, in the direction of St. Mary's Church, was taken from the antethreshold of number 31, almost under St. Mary's Gate, leading to the Long Riverside. Turning around, you can see on the inner wall of the gate, on the town side, a stone with Gdańsk's coat of arms. It comes from the time of the Teutonic Order, as the crest does not include the crown above the crosses.

50

The beginning of Mariacka Street, closed off by the eastern wall of the presbyterium of the St. Mary's Church. The portal below the slender window is located on the axis of the northern aisle of the presbyterium. The first house on Mariacka Street is also the oldest surviving house. Although all of the houses are of an earlier date, only this one has retained the gothic elevation divided by sharply-pointed niches and the stepped and crenellated summit. This is a modest house with only two axes on the elevation and the remaining walls not of brick, but of a skeletal construction. The next house on the left is much more imposing, albeit with a modest facade enlivened only by large windows. It comes from the XVII century and was built from the small bricks known as pantiles which were popular at the time.

51

The same house - number 2 - but now in the centre of the photograph. In the foreground we notice two vertical posts at the sides of the stairs leading up to the terrace of number 1 Mariacka Street. These facing stones are the original forms of the later richly artistic decoration of the famous Gdańsk antethresholds. The flag-stones seen by the sides of the antethreshold stairs of this house were reconstructed on the basis of fragments in the National Museum, dating from the first quarter of the XVI century, and found in the debris near number 26 Chlebnicka Street. In the background we can see a mannerist house from 1608 with authentic fragments of the portal and reconstructed baroque antethreshold.

52

The entire north side of Mariacka Street from the Basilica to the gate, leading to the Motława. Here we can easily see the lively rhythm of the narrow town-houses and the antethresholds which seem to be forming layers, one upon the other, in the perspective of the street. The antethresholds have a variety of balustrades, as well as different shapes of posts either by the steps or in front of them. The first of these houses, in the mannerist style from 1569, has a baroque antethreshold from the end of the XVII century. The stones laid here were partly restored and are open-carved with the motifs characteristic for that time of plants and animals.

53

At number 6 on the opposite, southern side of Mariacka Street is a house with a mannerist elevation faced with brick, and embellished with detailed carvings in stone: in the mouldings and in the fluting around the large rectangular windows. From the same period, around 1600, comes the impressive and very beautiful portal of measured proportions, with fluted Tuscan pilasters and with frugal application of rollwork ornamentation, almost classical in its character and appearance. The date above the portal - 1752 - refers to the antethreshold with its late baroque-rococo features. It is worth emphasising that all the posts and flag-stones of this antethreshold are authentic. The stones present personifications of two virtues, the depiction of certain abstract ideas in the form of female figures: on the left Castitas, purity with a palm-branch; on the right Spes, hope with a dove, a hive with bees, and a bunch of poppies and ears of corn. On the posts are asymmetric compositions of ornamental acanthus and rocaille.

54

The northern side of Mariacka Street in the middle section, between the two streets - Krowia (Cow) and Grząska (Muddy) - which cross here at right angles to Mariacka Street.

55

The opposite, southern, side of Mariacka Street, between the same two streets, beginning from the classical antethreshold of the almost invisible house at number 9, which is in the transitional style between rococo and classicism. The next house, number 10, with a classical facade from 1843, has a mannerist portal from the first quarter of the XVII century and a late baroque-regency antethreshold from the first quarter of the XVIII century. House number 12 has a facade characteristic of late gothic with deep chiaroscuro niches, and with a clearly separated high ground floor housing the vestibule. The neighbouring houses - numbers 11 and 13 - have early baroque elevations from the middle of the XVII century.

56-57

The town-house at 3 Mariacka Street is on the corner of one of two narrow side-streets: Klesza Street. For this reason the balustrade not only fences off the front of the antethreshold but also forms the side wall. Consequently the arrangement of flagstones is greater - we can see here cupids with bunches of flowers and grapes. From the front the cupids are playing games of love - they are firing off their arrows and are consoling each other when the arrows break.

58

The northern side of Mariacka Street: the whole eastern stretch from Grząska Street to Mydlarska Street (Soap Street) and St. Mary's Gate.

59

Mariacka Street - the last of the row of houses on the northern side: in the foreground the rococo antethreshold of number 33; in the middle number 30, in the late-mannerist style, with a portal of fine stonework, decorated with shells and acanthus and with a classical antethreshold from 1764; the last house, on the corner, is number 28 and is from about 1760. It has rococo features and modest forms.

60

The eastern fragment of Mariacka Street where it heads off towards the port on the Motława in the direction of the Long Riverside up to the gate which closes off the street. The gate, and the Naturalists' House on the right dominating with its mass and with its characteristic turret, are the premises of the Archaeological Museum.

61

The silhouette of St. Mary's Church, seen from the east, from the area between Mariacka Street and Chlebnicka Street, seems to appear from amidst the greenery. The upper part of the church, with its summits and lofty turrets seems to rise and float above the ordinary domestic buildings.

62

In the northern part of the complex of buildings of St. Mary's presbytery, next to Holy Ghost Street, the baroque shape of the Royal Chapel dominates. It could easily be imagined that this is the fronton of the church, with its three portals and three large windows, generously illuminating the interior, and with the cupola over the central inner area. The whole facade is flanked by two small town-houses with baroque-shaped summits. The chapel, therefore, despite the monumental form of its classical baroque, so alien to the local tradition, seems to melt into the town buildings and become one with them. In reality the whole church is oriented, and is therefore situated parallel to the street. The formal fronton, divided by Ionic pilasters of great order, of veritably palatial character, masks the central nave of the church which is square in plan. Behind the facades of the houses are the presbyterium on the left side and the porch on the right, western side. The church itself has its liturgical area on a higher level; the gate and the door on the ground floor constitute the entrance to the presbytery close.
This unusual structure mirrors the complexity of religious relations in old Gdańsk. When the Catholics were finally deprived in 1573 of the right to use St. Mary's Church by the more numerous Protestants, the kings of Poland, wanting to extend their protection, did not resign from their right of patronage over the shrine and continued to maintain the Catholic parish priest. It was only during a longer visit to Gdańsk by Jan III Sobieski

from August 1677 to February 1678 in connection with preparations for war with Prussia that plans guaranteeing the Catholics a place of worship of their own were realised. The direct impulse was provided by the bequest of 80,000 guilders left by the primate archbishop of Gniezno, Andrzej Olszowski, after his death on 29 August 1677. The king, as the founder and executor, added a further 20,000 guilders. The only possible place for the building was the area of the presbytery, outside the jurisdiction of the town. The patrons of both the generous benefactors - St. John the Baptist and St. Andrew the Apostle - were accepted, together with the Holy Ghost, as patrons of the church. The author of the project was most probably Tylman van Gameren, the fashionable architect, active chiefly in the Warsaw area, and with many commissions from the king and his retinue. He represented the classical trend in baroque architecture. As a military architect he would undoubtedly have accompanied the king on his journey to Gdańsk. Because of the then dense development around St. Mary's Church, the northern elevation was the only one to which it was possible to give a representational scenic facade. It lies near the relatively wide Holy Ghost Street and is opposite the entrance to Grobla Street (Weir Street), which runs across the Main Town. This created the opportunity for a splendid architectural effect, accordant with the aesthetic principles of baroque. The building of the Chapel was supervised from 1678 to 1681 by the Gdańsk builder and building entrepreneur Bartel Ranisch. He should also be credited with the obvious deviations from classical restraint in this work in favour of greater decorative and artistic effect. The author and executor of the decoration of the facade was the sculptor Andrzej Schluter the younger (1659-1714), active later in Warsaw, where he collaborated with Tylman van Gameren, and later as an architect in Berlin and St. Petersburg.

63

The portal of the central gate, leading to the close of the presbytery of St. Mary's Church, supported by Ionic columns, and with a divided pediment. The restrained serious architecture has been relieved by artistic ornament: acanthus leaves, garlands, festoons, scrolls, heads of angels, and shells.

64

The central cupola on an octagonal tambour and with two small cupola lanterns. By a minimal amount they have been placed a little forward - in this way the plan views have been varied and a typical baroque dynamism of composition has been achieved. At the same time the elements are definitely classical, in that they refer both to ancient forms and to renaissance ones. Above the middle window has been placed a cartouche with the crest of the Polish Republic, with the coat of arms of Jan III Sobieski in the central field.

65

The intended effect of competition between the Royal Chapel and St. Mary's Church can be seen when we look at both buildings from Grobla Street. From there the baroque elevation, in palatial style, seems to superimpose itself on to the mass of the gothic parish church with its decoratively treated summits on the northern transept, flanked by slender many-sided turrets. On the crown of the left summit a clock has been placed high enough to inform the inhabitants of the passage of time in an age when the possession of a watch would have been a rarity.

66-67

The decoration of the central archway of the portal of the Royal Chapel, with garlands and festoons, bunches of flowers and fruit, and acanthus leaves, all intertwined and turning into shells.

68

Holy Ghost Street - one of the wide streets perpendicular to the Motława and runing across the whole Main Town, whose both ends at one time were closed off by gates: in the west, on the land side, by the Ludwisarsaka Gate (Foundry Gate), and on the port side by the Holy Ghost Gate, recently rebuilt on the basis of surviving fragments. The modest rectangular building in the background, whose elevation is enlivened only by the rows of windows, is far from the rich divisions of other water-gates. During the rebuilding of the town after the destruction of the last war, only the north side of the street was reconstructed with a whole row of antethresholds. On the photograph can be seen in the foreground the antethresholds of number 81 to 85: the first is rococo, then classical, baroque from 1713 and 1690, and regency. It was decided not to rebuild the row of houses opposite, which allowed for the creation of more green spaces and greater access of sunlight to the houses. The remnants of the antethresholds on the southern side easily allow us to see where the original buildings stood and to imagine their density, so characteristic of rich and dynamic towns of traders and craftsmen.

69

This partly destroyed and cracked flag-stone from the antethreshold of a Gdańsk house is from the last century, but it is a reference to XVIII century forms. It has been relaid in the path which runs along the line of unreconstructed antethresholds on the south side of Holy Ghost Street. The ship with difficulty overcoming the stormy waves is here a symbol of the wealth of Gdańsk and of the source of that wealth, a symbol of doggedness and hard work, and the enterprise of its inhabitants, not frightened of difficulty and risk.

70

Holy Ghost Street - the view in the evening looking west from the antethreshold of number 86, with the mass of St. Mary's Basilica and the Royal Chapel outlined against the sky.

71

St. Mary's Church also in the evening seen from Mariacka Street, with the rays of the setting sun still shining through the windows of the Basilica.

72

The antethreshold of 116 Holy Ghost Street, lying near the Motława at the eastern end of the street. The flag-stones and posts are covered in boldly carved rocaille ornamentation and the rococo portal of this house has also been preserved. In the background can be seen the antethreshold of the neighbouring house, number 115, with a stone on which is portrayed the prophet Daniel in the lions' den (c.f. photograph 74).

73

A fragment of the late baroque antethreshold of 110 Holy Ghost Street.

74

A flag-stone from the antethreshold of 115 Holy Ghost Street, of irregular shape, typical of the late baroque and rococo period, portraying Job lying on a dung-heap. Together with the second stone shown on photograph 72, this shows a biblical scene, whose general idea is total faith in God, in His word, despite setbacks and apparent paradoxes.

A fragment of a baroque post with an ornamental cherub's head, now placed in the antethreshold of 117 Holy Ghost Street, but originally from number 59 on the same street.

76

The parish church of St. John was built on wet ground near the Motława between the Main Town and the Teutonic Castle on land designated for building quite late - in the second half of the XIV century. Originally a small chapel stood here, then a larger basilica church, a branch of St. Catherine's Church in the Old Town. The building of the present church, or rather the rebuilding of the earlier one into a church with a nave, two aisles and a transept, took place in the second half of the XIV century and the first half of the XV century. The vaulting of the interior was completed between 1463 and 1465. The tower which is so dominant on the photograph (c.f. photograph 84) was also built in several stages. Because of the instability of the ground, and because the foundations were too weak for this kind of terrain, the church is in danger of collapse.
The significance of this church is increased by the fact that - despite wartime damage - most of the interior, dating primarily from the XVII century, has been preserved. The fittings have been scattered to many places, but most of them, for example the organ and the pulpit, have been utilised in St. Mary's Church. In the burned - out church a museum conserving stones and stone fragments has been established. In situ has remained the main stone altar, the work of Abraham van den Blocke from 1611.

77

At the eastern end of Szeroka Street, near the Crane, an impressive late gothic town-house (number 75) draws the attention - it has a characteristic brick facade, divided by profiled pillars close to the wall, and crowned with an attic summit. It is, however, a reconstruction. The house was rebuilt in later years but during the post - 1945 reconstruction the restorers decided to restore the building to its medieval form from the beginning of the XVI century. The house was rebuilt on the basis of surviving fragments and of traces in the structure of the walls. On the left is a town-house of undoubted late gothic pedigree, with large windows typical of the Dutch mannerist style, but without decoration and with a classical summit. On the right is a small house with baroque features but with a gothic core.

78

Piwna Street has beautiful scenic views at both its ends. At its western end there is the Great Armoury (photograph 79). Looking from the Armoury in the opposite direction we can see, rising above the compact row of narrow town-houses with their lively rhythm of windows and summits, the massive and majestically tall tower of St. Mary's Church. Piwna Street is slightly crescent-shaped, which makes it even more picturesque and varied. This irregularity may have come from the need to adapt the road to the existing older buildnigs, during the relocations of 1342-1346. The second reason may have been the need to adapt the road to the uncommonly large size of St. Mary's Church which does not stand on a designated square but is surrounded by densely packed domestic dwellings. When it passes the church, Piwna Street becomes Chlebnicka Street and goes down to the Motława.

79

The western end of Piwna Street is closed off by the magnificent wide facade of the Great Armoury, visible from far down the street. The building of the Armoury was incorporated into the line of the defensive wall (to accommodate it one of the gothic towers had to be demolished) in 1601-1605 and some of the final details were not completed until 1609. The ground floor, where were stored the heavy weapons, artillery and ammunition, was designed as a wide four-naved hall supported by 15 granite pillars. This interior division is echoed in the shape of the facade, which resembles four town-houses. In contrast to the rear elevation on the Targ Drzewny (Wood Market) side (photograph 85 and engraving 17 on p. 23), where this four-segment structure is strongly accented, the fronton gives a different impression: against the background of both side segments have been added tall towers inside which are the staircases; between the summits of both central segments attic walls have been added. On the ground floor two mighty portals give easy access to the hall on the lower level. The whole facade, equally divided by large rectangular windows, is richly decorated with artistic figures and ornaments carved in stone and concentrated particularly on the portals, in the summits and attics and on the central axis. We can recognise here the figure of Athene, figures of warriors, elements of arms, so-called panoplies, the crests of Gdańsk and the characteristic rollwork ornament of Dutch mannerism. Overall, despite the military and utilitarian designation of this building, an elegant effect has been achieved, and thanks to the richness and variety of the forms, and the overcoming of the additionality of the members, a monumental, even palatial, character has been achieved for the building. The towers already mentioned wonderfully integrate the whole facade into the panorama of Piwna Street. One can see here the hand of an experienced architect, consciously shaping not only the form of the elevation, but also an element arranging a large part of the area of the town.

The author of the project accepted by the Town Council in 1599 was Anthony van Obberghen. The building works were directed by Jan Strakowski, while the execution of the elevation of the fronton was entrusted to Abraham van den Blocke. The Dutch origins of the architectural and decorative forms do not give rise to any doubts, particularly in view of the great similarity to the graphic designs of Jan Vredeman de Vries, from the third quarter of the XVI century. De Vries himself, towards the end of his busy and overworked life, was active also in Gdańsk, as has already been mentioned (c.f. photograph 18).

80

The northern side of Piwna Street, as seen on photograph 78, has had its antethresholds restored. On this photograph we can see two of them, baroque ones, from numbers 59 and 60. The first is from 1660 and is one of the earliest baroque antethresholsd in Gdańsk - here it has been added to a mannerist facade and portal from 1617. The second is late baroque, from about 1700, with cupids, and is largely restored.

81

One of the flagstones from the antethreshold of number 1 Piwna Street (c.f. photograph 82). The rococo stones laid here are from the middle of the XVIII century and include the representation of ruined classical architecture, repeated in two variations.

82

The first houses on Piwna Street, on the corner of Tkacka Street (Weavers' Street), seen from the Great Armoury. Between the two town-houses with baroque summits can be seen an impressive house in the mannerist-early baroque style, with a richly decorated and divided facade, probably the work of Andrzej Schluter the elder from 1638-1640.

83

The last fragment of Chlebnicka Street, with the houses almost touching the southern elevation of St. Mary's Church. In the distance is Piwna Street.

84

The north-western district of the Main Town, from a bird's-eye view, from the tower of St. Mary's Church, bounded by the following streets: Szeroka, Grobla and Podwale Staromiejskie (Old Town Ramparts), and lying along the Motława. This part of the town, because of the wet terrain, was not settled until the XIV century. In the middle rises the brick mass of St. John's Church, with its nave, two aisles and transept (c.f. photograph 76). In the background is Lead Island, the last bend of the Motława, and finally the shipyard and port of Gdańsk on the banks of the Vistula.

85

The western elevation of the Great Armoury, seen from Targ Drzewny (c.f. the engraving from Curicke's work, on p. 23). Here we can easily see the segmentalisation of this building, as if it were composed of four town-houses. This side of the Arsenal does not possess such an elegant character as the facade on Piwna Street - after all it used to look out onto a minor square on the outskirts of the town. Despite this, it preserves the monumental nature of the whole and the analogous decoration on the summits. Powder was stored in the neighbouring many-sided gothic Słomiana Baszta (Straw Tower) which was linked to the Arsenal by a covered pathway. In the free-standing building on the opposite, northern side, which has not survived, but which is visible on the engraving in Curicke's work, the cannon-balls were cast. Because these cannon-balls were jokingly referred to as pills, the building was called the Old Apothecary's. Currently in the Armoury are the premises of the Fine Arts Academy, for whose needs a new building was constructed on the south side - a building not in keeping with the local architectural tradition and constituting a foreign, aggressive intrusion into the panorama of the town.

86

The Upland Gate, constructed from 1574 to 1576, is the first external element of the rebuilt western gate complex leading to Long Street and to the centre of the Main Town. It was built at the same time as the ring of modern bastion fortifications and was set in the earthworks running in front of the gothic defensive walls. The earthworks were levelled in 1895, as a result of which the gate now stands by itself on a spacious square (c.f. the engraving in Curicke's work, reproduced on p. 21, and the commentary to photograph 16). For the first ten years after its construction the gate was unadorned. Finally in 1586 the Town Council commissioned Willem van den Blocke to add decorations. The elevation of the gate is the first of this artist's works in Gdańsk - his work, like that of his two sons Abraham and Isaac, had a decisive impact on the shape and style of the art of Gdańsk at the end of the XVI and beginning of the XVII centuries. The gate, thanks to the genius of the architect and sculptor, unites in itself the need for appropriate elegance as well as the defensive qualities necessary in this type of building. The massive lower level, so like a fortress in character, has renaissance-mannerist Italianate forms, while the upper part, with its marked artistic decoration, is Dutch mannerist, with its love of an abundance of abstract ornamental forms. The upper part is also a heraldic frieze: the coats of arms of the Polish Republic, the Kingdom of Prussia, and Gdańsk are placed in the cartouches made from rollwork. The crests are supported by, in turn, pairs of angels, unicorns and lions. The Latin inscriptions call for public life to be based on justice and piety, and for peace, freedom and agreement, as well as for union with the Republic: IUSTITIA ET PIETAS DUO SUNT REGNORUM OMNIUM FUNDAMENTA. CIVITATIBUS HAEC OPTANDA BONA MAXIMAE: PAX, LIBERTAS, CONCORDIA and SAPIENTISSIMAE SUNT OMNIA QUAE PRO REPUBLICA FIUNT. (Two are the bases of great kingdoms: justice and piety. Peace, liberty and agreement - these are the things most desired by all states. The wisest are the things which are done for the Republic). The Upland Gate marks the beginning of the Royal Way. It was through here that all official guests, all ambassadors, and all the royal processions entered Gdańsk. In the distance we can see the fortified ante-gate of the Long Street Gate, with the gothic gate rebuilt as the Torture House with the Prison Tower, and beyond that but not seen on this photograph the Golden Gate (see photograph 88). In this way on the small square by the Coal Market and by the main entrance to the town are gathered in close proximity three outstanding works of mannerist architecture, some of the finest in northern Europe, and all of them with a military function.

87

The Court of the Brotherhood of St. George takes its beginnings from the conflict which arose between this brotherhood, the oldest merchants' association in Gdańsk and one which cultivated elitism, exclusivity and chivalric traditions, and other brotherhoods, or "benches", which used the new Arthur's Court (c.f. commentary to photograph 19). To the conflict arising from uncomfortable proximity was added in 1486 the tournament crisis: the traditional tournament was not won by a representative of the patrician class but by the son of a peasant. The patricians in the knightly Brotherhood of St. George decided to break away. The building of the new seat , next to the brotherhood's shooting-range between the walls near the Long Street Gate, was begun in 1487 and completed in 1494. This building, albeit quite small, is on an almost square base and is one of the most valuable architectural monuments in Gdańsk: the excellent design, the blending with the surroundings, the splendid feeling for the form of the mass and the division of the elevation, the lightness, the elegance, the expressiveness of the form. In this building we can see the influences of Flemish late gothic architecture, and at the same time links with the local tradition (c.f. the engraving in Curicke's chronicle, engraving 10 on p. 16). The figure of St George on the top of the building is from 1566. The Court was used by the brotherhood until it was dissolved in 1798.

88

The Court of the Brotherhood of St. George was joined at its corner to the Long Street Gate in its original gothic form. To protect better this main entrance to the town from the land side, a fortified ante-gate together with the Prison Tower was built in about 1380 and modernised and improved in late years. The loss of the military function of the Long Street Gate was completed with the creation of the earthworks which incorporated the Upland Gate (c.f. photograph 86), which in turn became the first gate in the western complex. Soon afterwards the modest Long Street Gate was replaced by a more elegant building adding appropriate lustre to the entrance to Gdańsk. The Golden Gate, so called because of the wealth of gilding, was built between 1612 and 1614 according to the design of Abraham van den Blocke by his collaborator Jan Strakowski. This in effect quite small edifice creates an uncommonly monumental impression because of its classical forms, the hierarchy of column orders, Ionic on the lower level and Corinthian on the upper, and the noble, harmonious proportions. In a way which raises no doubts, the whole is a reference to Roman triumphal arches, which of course performed a similar function. The ideological programme is completed by the figures placed on the balustrade, personifications of Peace, Liberty, Wealth and Fame, as well as the inscription (in German) on the frieze between the levels which is a fragment of Psalm 122 calling for peace and good fortune for Jerusalem as the Town of God, and in turn for Gdańsk, as the town chosen by God and endowed with His mercy: "May they enjoy peace who love you. May peace reign in these walls, and contentment in your palaces" (translated by Roman Brandstaetter). The statues placed on the Long Street side (c.f. the engraving from Curicke's chronicle, engraving 18 on p.24) represent virtues, thanks to which it is possible to achieve the state suggested to the traveller arriving in the town: the "inner" statues represent: Caution, Piety, Justice and Agreement, while the Latin inscription on the frieze adds: CONCORDIA RESPUBLICAE PARVAE

CRESCUNT DISCORDIA MAGNE CONCIDUNT (Through agreement do small states grow, through discord do large ones fall). These statues were erected in 1647 by Piotr Ringering, then in 1880 they were taken down and they disappeared. During the reconstruction of 1957 they were recreated according to the engravings of Jeremias Falck the XVII century Gdańsk engraver who called himself Falck Polonus. The engravings were made in 1648-1649 and faithfully reproduce Ringering's originals.

89

The statue of Jan III Sobieski in the Wood Market on the border of the Main Town and the Old Town. The statue is a symbol of Poland's most recent history - it was cast in bronze according to the design of Tadeusz Barącz (in 1897 according to the date on the plinth) and erected, before Poland regained independence, on the Hetman's Ramparts in Lwów from where in 1945 it was taken and placed in the park of the former king's summer residence in Wilanów. In 1965 the statue was once again unveiled, this time in Gdańsk, to underline the old and recently renewed links between Poland and Gdańsk and to emphasise the king's links with the town. In the background we can see the western summit and the turret of the Dominican Church of St. Nicholas.

90

The Church of St. Nicholas seen from the distant perspective of Świętojańska Street (St John's Street), from the church of the same name (c.f. Schultz's similar view - engraving 2 on p. 6). The Dominicans were brought to Gdańsk from Cracow in 1227 by Prince Świętopełk, who assigned to them the already existing wooden church of St Nicholas, which served as the parish church for the market and craft settlement on the land later attached to the Main Town. The Dominicans immediately started to build a new church, which has not survived, but on whose foundations were later built the southern wall of the sacristy crowned with crenelles. The present church was built in 1340-1380 and has a nave and two aisles with an elongated presbyterium for the use of the convent. This part was once separated from the body of the nave, which was for the faithful, with the help of a reading-room. Despite the advances of the reformation in the XVI century, despite riots, despite the aversion not to say persecution from the Protestant part of the middle classes and the Protestant Council, the Dominicans survived in Gdańsk until the order was disbanded by the Prussian authorities in 1835 and the church remained at all times Catholic. The Dominicans returned after the war in 1945. The church survived the damage done to the town in 1945 without any great harm. The architectural mass of the church survived, as did the interiors, which is an astounding fact considering the sea of ruins that was the historic centre of Gdańsk.

91

The earlier established Old Town did not play such a significant role later as did the Main Town, which gathered to itself all the patricians and rich merchant classes. We can, however, find even in this part of the town a whole group of monuments which are interesting and worth our attention. Among these is undoubtedly the Church of St. Bridget, and not only because of its past and its architectural features, but also on account of the role played by this church in Poland's most recent history. The group of people who were associated with this shrine and with the Ministry of the Sea which is based here were instrumental in the process of the democratisation of life in Poland. In the place of the present church once stood the chapel of St. Mary Magdalen, belonging to penitents who led their communal life here. The decisive moment came with the exposition here of the body of St. Bridget of Sweden, which was carried through Gdańsk in 1374. St. Bridget was canonised in 1391. In 1396 some of the penitents accepted the rules established by St. Bridget in about 1346 for the convent in Vadsten. It is worth emphasising that apart from the parent establishment the Gdańsk convent is among the three oldest convents of St. Bridget, along with Florence and Rome. The building of the church was quickly begun. The building originally had a nave and an aisle but in 1514 a southern nave and a presbyterium on the western side were added. This was not the usual custom but it did accord with the rules of the order. The late gothic crystalline vaulting was added in the reconstruction after the fire of 1587. Soon afterwards, in 1616, a renaissance bell-tower was built on the south-eastern corner. The tower gained a baroque cupola in 1678, designed by Piotr Willer, the presumed author of the engravings illustrating the Gdańsk Chronicles of Reinhold Curicke. The church was burned and damaged towards the end of the war and lost its rich baroque interiors among other things. It stood in ruins until 1970 when it was returned to the Diocese of Gdańsk. Reconstructed, the church harmoniously reconciles within itself its gothic architecture and the modern interior decoration. This photograph was taken from the corner of the presbyterium of the church of St. Catherine.

92

The church of St. Catherine - the parish church for the Old Town - part of the body of the nave and the tower seen from the north, from beyond the Radunia Canal. Later tradition and historiography of Gdańsk place the beginning of this church in 1185. This is not however very likely. Rather more probable is that the church was founded and built immediately after the first parish church of St. Nicholas was given to the Dominicans in 1227 (see photograph 90). The first mention of the church of St. Catherine comes from 1263. The present church was built in several stages from the beginning of the presbyterium in 1326 to the raising of the tower in 1485. The beautiful richly divided baroque cupola, consciously intended to compete with the tower of the Main Town Hall, was built in 1634. Already in the XVI century a carillion was installed in the tower and it was later enlarged. The bells, together with the cupola, melted in the fire of 1905 which was caused by lightning, and the restored bells were taken to Lubeck in 1842. In 1945 the church was seriously damaged - even the rich interior and fittings were partly destroyed. In 1947 the Carmelites took over the burned-out church and for many years worked on reconstructing it and restoring it as a place of worship. Finally in 1989, to emphasise the fact that the restoration was complete, a peal of 37 bells was heard once again from the church. In this church, along with many other valuable items, can be found the tomb of the great Gdańsk scientist and astronomer Jan Heweliusz who died in 1687. On this photograph, on the right, is visible the Small Mill on the Radunia Canal built in the XIV century and restored after the war.

93

The southern wall of the House of the Pelplin Abbots on the Radunia Canal. This town-house comes from 1612 and although it was restored in 1912 it survived the war undamaged. It is one of the best examples in Gdańsk of brick and stone building in the mannerist style influenced by Dutch architecture. The best evidence for this is the facade, not shown on the photograph. Uncommon charm is added to this building by the vines which are growing on the entire side elevation.

94

One of the most picturesque corners of Gdańsk: the Radunia Canal, with the Great Mill and the tower of St. Catherine's Church visible in the background closing off the view. The digging of a new channel for the Radunia Stream in 1338-1356 allowed for the redirecting of its course through the Old Town and for the establishment on its banks of many industrial premises: there was a tannery, a fullery for furs and cloth, a copper forge, a sawmill and grindery, an oil-mill and mill for grinding cereals. Above all, however, from the benefits of its dammed current profited the numerous grain mills. On the left we can see the extreme end of the side wall of the House of the Pelplin Abbots: on this autumnal photograph the vines have taken on a fiery golden-red hue.

he Radunia Canal seen from the opposite direction, from east to west from the bridge on the extension of Ślusarska Street (Ironworkers' Street); in the background is St. Catherine's Church.

n a certain place, close to St. Catherine's Church, the Radunia Canal forks and forms an island, the better to make use of its current. Among the mills functioning here the biggest and most famous is the Great Mill, which has 18 mill wheels, and which was built in the middle of the XIV century when it brought great profits to the Teutonic Order to which it belonged. After 1454 it was presented to the town by King Kazimierz IV Jagiellończyk. Compare the reproduction from Curicke's work on p. 13 with its presentation of the working mill from the opposite, eastern, side where the ovens for baking bread were situated.

he western summit of the former Franciscan church, the Holy Trinity. The Franciscans came to Gdańsk relatively late, in 1419, and settled in a less exposed place than other orders - in the Old Suburb. The building of the church and the friary was begun in 1431 with the presbyterium. The work lasted until the beginning of the XIV century, not only because the plans were changed but also because of a building disaster which took place in 1503. The church is late gothic in form, which can be seen inside in the type, variety and drawing of the network and crystalline vaulting. On the outside the decorative forms of the architecture and the ornamentation are most apparent in the delicate but vibrant crowned summits, contrasting with the great plain walls of the massive body of the church. This photograph presents the triple summits of the western elevation, matching the nave and aisles covered with their individual roofs. With the advance of the reformation in Gdańsk, evangelical services were introduced early in the Church of the Holy Trinity, and the friary was taken over by the Town Council in 1555. In the chapel of St. Anne, which had been added in 1484, evangelical sermons were preached in Polish from 1552. From 1558 a secondary school functioned in the friary, ten years later called a grammar school, and later still the Academic Grammar School, famous for its high level of learning. Near the Grammar School was the Town Council Library, whose interior is presented on the engraving on p. 26 from the work of Reinhold Curicke.

he Old Town Hall, between the Great Mill and the former Carmelite church of St Joseph. The photograph was taken from the opposite bank of the Radunia into whose waters gazes this small but harmoniously composed building, once splendidly integrated with its surroundings, which cannot now be appreciated. The Town Hall was built in 1587-1589. The authorship of the project can with certainty be ascribed to Anthony van Obberghen. This was the first work of this outstanding artist in Gdańsk (c.f. photographs 79 and 85). Compared with the Great Armoury the economical decoration is striking, as is the noble restraint. The work does however realise all the most important postulates of Dutch mannerism: the contrast of the stone and brick elevation, the precisely sculpted detail, the large windows densely divided internally, the contrast between the severe cubic mass and the slender vertical corner turrets which seem to foretell the tall and richly divided central cupola, sited without a tower directly on the crest of the roof. It is a modest building but uncommonly shapely and charming. The historical and artistic features of the Town Hall are enhanced by the fact that the building was virtually unaffected by the war. The interior of the Town Hall was substantially rebuilt in 1911-1914 in the neo-renaissance style. At the same time a collection was started of interesting artistic relics from various Gdańsk patrician town-houses which were undergoing modernisation and rebuilding. In this way many valuable items were saved, for example a renaissance portal, or a three-arched wall from about 1560 from the great vestibule of the so-called Konert House at 45 Long Street opposite the Main Town Hall and with its side elevation on The Long Market, of all Gdańsk town-houses the one closest to the norms of classical renaissance art. In the interiors of the Town Hall can also be found two uncommonly valuable pictures painted by Gdańsk artists in the middle of the XVII century: a painting with an allegorical theme ascribed to Herman Han, and a representation of Sybil by Adolf Boy.

99

The last view of the Long Riverside, of Gdańsk's old port, stretching the whole length of the Main Town from Cow Gate to the Fish Market. The photograph was taken at dawn from the bridge between Podwale Przedmiejskie (Suburban Ramparts) and Granary Island, when the town, still sleeping, solitary and completely silent, is reflected in the calm mirror of the Motława.

100

The Crane, seen in duplicate because of its reflection in the waters of the Motława with its sharp silhouette in the light of the setting sun. "The Crane, with the heavy silhouette of its head, calmly poised above the busy current of port activity on the Motława" (Jan Kilarski, 1947), became the sign, the symbol of Gdańsk, its proud and rich trading past, its modern historic and artistic significance, its attractiveness for tourists. The granaries opposite on Lead Island are also reflected in the water - the three already mentioned (Oliwski, Miedź and Panna - c.f. photograph 4) which make up together with the Crane the complex of Maritime Museum buildings - and the Royal Granary just visible further off, situated in different relation than the others to the current of the river, not with its summit but with its ridge. The building of the Royal Granary was started by Abraham van den Blocke before 1606, and it was finished by Jan Strakowski in 1621. This granary, built to store grain from the king's lands, was to have been built by the town as early as 1454. In the still calm of the evening, this old Gdańsk, despite terrible destruction, as if to spite history, stubbornly goes on.

101

The row of newly restored granaries on Granary Island between the Green Bridge and the Podwale Przedmiejskie Bridge. At one time would moor here specially constructed flat-bottomed boats from the Vistula, from which in late summer and autumn would be unloaded grain to the granaries. To the wooden Long Landing-stage (Długi Pomost) would come in spring the following year sea vessels, primarily flying the Dutch flag, to take the grain to western European countries which had troubles in supplying adequate amounts of food to their own populations. It does not need adding how much the price of corn would increase during the period of storage. Here in fact is the source of the great wealth of old Gdańsk - here is the basis of Gdańsk's role as intermediary between the Republic and the west.

102

This is where our journey around old Gdańsk began and with the silhouette of Gdańsk seen from beyond the Motława from the Stągiewna Gate will we say farewell to a town of hundreds of town-houses, households of industrious and thrifty merchants and craftsmen, a town of towers shooting high into the air, marking its pride, its power and its significance.

MONUMENTS OF ART AND CULTURE OF NORTHERN POLAND

Editorial Committee of the Series:

WACŁAW GÓRSKI
MAREK ŻAK
MICHAŁ WOŹNIAK

VOLUME II GDAŃSK

Text: **Lech Krzyżanowski**
Edition and commentaries on the illustrations: **Michał Woźniak**
Translation: © **FAST Gdańsk**
Photographs: **Wacław Górski, Marek Żak**
Photograph 84: **Jaromir Nowak**

Typesetting: **FAST Gdańsk**

Sources of Illustrations:

© 1996 by Oficyna Wydawnicza „Excalibur"
ISBN 83-903431-5-0
Printed in Poland 2000

Oficyna Wydawnicza „Excalibur"
ul. Koralowa 4
85–837 Bydgoszcz

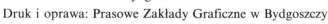 Druk i oprawa: Prasowe Zakłady Graficzne w Bydgoszczy